THE SLIGO, LEITRIM & NORTHERN COUN RAILWAY

An Irish Railway Pictorial

Neil Sprinks

Midland Publishing

The Sligo, Leitrim & Northern Counties
Railway: An Irish Railway Pictorial
© 2001 Neil Whitby Sprinks

ISBN 1 85780 112 1

Published in 2001 by Midland Publishing
4 Watling Drive, Hinckley, Leics.
LE10 3EY, England.
Tel: 01455 254 490 Fax: 01455 254 495
E-mail: midlandbooks@compuserve.com

Design concept and layout
© Midland Publishing and
Stephen Thompson Associates.

Midland Publishing is an imprint of
Ian Allan Publishing Ltd.

Printed in England by Ian Allan Printing Ltd
Molesey Road, Hersham, Surrey, KT12 4RG.

Front cover: **On 22nd June 1956,**
Lough Melvin, **one of the final series of
Sligo, Leitrim & Northern Counties Railway
Beyer Peacock-built 0-6-4Ts, approaches
the line's midway point and engineering
centre, Manorhamilton, with the 2.15pm
goods from Enniskillen to Sligo.** Peter Gray

Title page: **The well laden afternoon
Enniskillen to Sligo goods train,
again hauled by a 'Lough' class 0-6-4T,
photographed on an early June day in
1956. The train is some two miles out of
Enniskillen, the line's junction with the
Great Northern Railway, and is heading for
Florencecourt, the first SLNCR station on
its 48 mile long journey to the west.** Author

DEDICATION

This book is dedicated to the men and women
who worked on the Sligo, Leitrim & Northern
Counties Railway. They worked on the line on
all days, at all hours and in all weathers to earn a
living for themselves and their families. In doing
so they provided not only a vital service for their
communities, but also much interest and enjoy-
ment for railway enthusiasts from far and wide.

INTRODUCTION

The Sligo, Leitrim & Northern Counties
Railway was one of Ireland's most distinctive lines. Although of standard 5ft 3in gauge, it
remained independent throughout its existence from 1879 to 1957 and was Ireland's last
privately owned common carrier railway. Its 42
miles and 50 chains route from Carrignagat
Junction, 5½ miles south of Sligo on the
Midland Great Western line to Dublin, to a
junction with the Great Northern Railway at
Enniskillen was undulating, with sharp curves,
steep gradients and numerous level crossings,
all legacies of building the line at minimum
cost and as close as possible to the contours of
the land.

Over this line the trains were, in living memory, railbuses, a modern railcar, and steam-
hauled goods, cattle, mixed or special
passenger workings. Most, latterly all, steam
locomotives were of the unusual 0-6-4 tank
type from one manufacturer, Beyer Peacock.
The locomotives carried only names, and were
never given numbers.

Financial stringency led to longevity of
equipment, and there were remarkable
anachronisms in rolling stock, signalling and
workshop practices. But despite shortage of
money, there were many signs of ingenuity
and enterprise such as the use of railbuses
from 1935, while in the difficult mid-1940's a
new modern railcar was ordered and the company started running lorry and bus services.
Then, a few years later, when two essential new
steam locomotives were required, Beyer
Peacock 0-6-4 tanks of course, as had been the
norm since 1882, they were procured through
hire purchase.

The Line's Beginnings
The SLNCR was promoted primarily by promi-
nent residents and landowners at the Sligo end
of the route, anxious not only to bring the ben-
efits of rail transport to the area to be served by
the line, but also, by linking with the Great
Northern at Enniskillen, to provide outlets for
livestock to the ports of Derry and Belfast in
addition to that provided to Dublin since 1862,
by the Midland Great Western line from Sligo.
Ironstone, iron ore and coal traffic from the
Lough Allen area also featured in the company's prospectus, although this locality lay some
way to the south and was never connected to
the SLNCR, but was eventually reached by the
Arigna branch of the Cavan & Leitrim Railway.
A branch from Arigna to the SLNCR at
Dromahair was mooted, however, in 1904.

There had been earlier schemes for railways
from Sligo to Enniskillen, including one via
Bundoran which materialised in 1866 only as
the Bundoran to Bundoran Junction line,
worked by the Irish North Western Railway and
later part of the Great Northern. The gap
between Bundoran and Sligo was never filled.

The bill authorising the Sligo, Leitrim &
Northern Counties Railway was enacted by the
Westminster parliament on 11th August 1875.
The Act also conferred running powers for the
company's trains over the MGWR from its Sligo
passenger station and Sligo Quay goods station to Carrignagat Junction, and over a short
length of Irish North Western Railway metals
into Enniskillen station. The INWR became
one of the constituents of the GNR before the
SLNCR line was built.

Construction
The authorised share capital was £200,000,
with borrowing powers of up to an additional
£100,000. There were problems not only in
raising the money, but in getting a contractor
to build the line at an affordable price.
Eventually, in March 1877, the Chairman and
Engineer both resigned and entered into a
partnership to build the line themselves, construction beginning later that year. By the end
of 1877, rolling stock, to be used initially on
construction, began to arrive at Enniskillen.
This included two Avonside 0-6-2 tanks, and in
the following March, the contractors' own
0-4-0T, later taken briefly into SLNCR stock.

The line was built from the Enniskillen end,
and was opened in stages, the first, from
Enniskillen as far as Belcoo (12¼ miles)
opened for freight on 12th February 1879 and
for passengers on 18th March 1879. The five
miles on to Glenfarne opened the following
New Year's Day and traffic on the seven and a
half miles thence to Manorhamilton commenced on 1st December 1880. On 1st
September 1881 the 16¾ miles section from
Manorhamilton to Collooney was opened, but
the opening of the final one and a quarter
miles on to Carrignagat Junction, to connect
the line with the Midland Great Western, was
delayed until 7th November 1882 because of
problems with the bridge over the Owenmore
River. The SLNCR paid for the cost of
Carrignagat Junction, the signal box and sig-
nalmens' cottages and the cost of doubling the
MGWR line for approximately one mile into
Ballysodare station. The MGWR line on to Sligo
from Ballysodare was already double track.
1882, the year when the SLNCR line was completed also saw the arrival of the first of the
Beyer Peacock 0-6-4Ts, a locomotive type that
was to dominate, and latterly monopolise, the
company's locomotive fleet. Finally, in 1883,
the SLNCR assumed the form in which it was
known with the completion of alterations at
Enniskillen which enabled trains to enter the
rebuilt Great Northern Railway station. Until
then a temporary platform outside the main
station had been used.

As the Act authorising the SLNCR which had
been passed in 1875, had allowed five years for
the completion of the line, a second Act had to
be obtained in 1880, authorising an extension
of the time for a further three years. This legislation also allowed the raising of further capital
of £40,000 and the borrowing of an additional
£20,000.

Financial Problems Begin

The 1880 Act's additional capital and borrowing powers reflected the fact that the line was costing more to build and equip than had been expected. Indeed, the financial position was such that one of the shareholders had taken on responsibility for the company's debt for the purchase of rolling stock. In 1882 the entire locomotive and rolling stock fleet was on hire from him. Furthermore, the borrowing powers under the original 1875 Act had been called upon to secure, soon after the first section of line opened in 1879, a loan of £100,000 from the Board of Works. Although traffic receipts were above operating costs when the line was opened throughout, they were insufficient to meet charges on this loan or costs for the hire of locomotives and rolling stock. A request for a further Board of Works loan to purchase the locomotives and rolling stock was refused and as early as 1890 debts were such that a Receiver was appointed. The Board of Works ordered an enquiry into the working and management of the line. Four years later, despite rising revenue, delays to repayments of the loan were such that the Treasury seriously considered selling the line to the MGWR and the GNR for £120,000. The two companies were willing to purchase the line and to divide operations at the midway point of Manorhamilton. Local interests were vehemently opposed to this plan as it would negate the competition between the SLNCR and MGWR for traffic in the Sligo area. In 1895 the company put forward to the Board of Works and the Treasury proposals for a financial reconstruction, a form of which was finally agreed to in 1897. By this, the burden of loan interest was eased, the SLNCR at last owned its locomotives and rolling stock and was taken out of receivership.

The Claremorris and Collooney Line

One of the reasons for the government's stalling from 1895 to 1897 on the question of a financial reconstruction was to see the effect on the SLNCR's revenues of the opening in 1895 of the line from Claremorris to Collooney and to what extent this line would generate additional traffic for forwarding over the SLNCR route. The Claremorris to Collooney line was initially promoted over a period of years by local interests with whom the Locomotive and Permanent Way Superintendent of the SLNCR had close connections. Indeed in 1882 he had tried, unsuccessfully, to persuade the SLNCR to secure running powers over the line. A draft agreement was even drawn up for the line to be worked by the SLNCR.

When the Claremorris to Collooney line was finally opened on 1st October 1895, it became part of the Waterford & Limerick Railway, becoming the final northern section of its long route from Limerick to Sligo which prompted the company to change its name to the Waterford, Limerick & Western Railway at the end of that year. The line joined the MGWR route to Sligo at Collooney Junction, three quarters of a mile south of the SLNCR's junction at Carrignagat. A 46-chain connection was built from the Waterford & Limerick's Collooney station, passing beneath the MGWR line, to the SLNCR's Collooney station. This spur was W&L property and that company also contributed to the cost of installing, operating and maintaining the junction with the SLNCR line. The spur was primarily used for the transfer of special goods trains between the two lines. The WL.&WR became part of the Great Southern & Western Railway in 1901. The use of the spur declined from the 1920s onwards.

The SLNCR was not only affected by the Claremorris to Collooney line's presence and traffic emanating from it, but by the help which the new line's promoters had received from both central and local government towards the cost of the line as a result of legislation dating from 1883, after the SLNCR had been completed and paid for. When seeking the financial reconstruction mentioned in earlier paragraphs, which was finally secured in 1897, the SLNCR put forward to the Treasury and the Board of Works the argument that the Sligo company was a more important undertaking than the Claremorris to Collooney line and that at least it should be accorded the financial advantages which the promoters of the Claremorris line had enjoyed. These amounted to an outright grant and guaranteed interest payments on the rest of the capital used to construct the line. The SLNCR directors openly stated that if the 1883 legislation had been foreseen, they would have postponed the building of their line until after it had come into effect.

The Lull Before The Storm

A comparatively settled period on the SLNCR appears to have ensued from the financial reconstruction of 1897 until the start of the First World War, which was to presage vast changes in transport, politics and trade which would affect the railway for the rest of its days. How fundamental were the changes can be seen from the fact that whereas from probably the 1920s, and certainly from the 1930s onwards, the railways were fighting for their survival, in the early 1900s new lines were still being actively promoted. Several schemes affected the SLNCR notably plans to build lines to exploit the Arigna coal reserves.

Everything Changes

As a consequence of the war, came government control. For the only time in its existence, the SLNCR lost control of its own affairs when, from January 1917 to mid-August 1921, the Irish railway companies, including the SLNCR were controlled by the Irish Railway Executive Committee. Under the committee there were significant improvements in staff wages and working conditions. For example, in 1917 the company's expenditure increased by £6,200. In the same year receipts increased by only £1,500. Compensation from the government amounted to £4,741.

Worse was to come on the political front. Agitation for self government for Ireland turned from the peaceful parliamentary activity of the pre-war years to violent insurrection in 1916. The popular reaction to the execution of the leaders of the 1916 rebellion led to agitation for a break with Britain in the south of Ireland. This was vigorously opposed by the unionist population of the north. The solution, reluctantly accepted by both sides, was the partition of Ireland which followed the signing of the Anglo-Irish Treaty in December 1921. The SLNCR now found itself straddling an international frontier. The administrative headquarters of the line, situated at Enniskillen in County Fermanagh and that part of the line as far as a point west of Belcoo station, were now in Northern Ireland, while the major part of the line, in the counties of Cavan, Leitrim and Sligo, including the engineering headquarters and workshops at Manorhamilton, were in the Irish Free State.

Dissatisfaction with partition among elements in the Irish Free State led to a Civil War there from 1922 to 1923. During this period there were numerous attacks on the railways of the twenty six counties. These spread to the SLNCR in the early months of 1923. Between Manorhamilton and Glenfarne, vehicles on an up train were destroyed by fire on 7th March, and another up train was derailed on 3rd April. Dromahair signal box was damaged by fire and that at Carrignagat Junction was burnt down on St. Patrick's Day. The disruption affected other railways in the area. On 10th January 1923, the MGWR station at Sligo was destroyed by fire and locomotives, at Sligo engine shed, including one belonging to the SLNCR, were sent careering down the incline from the station to Sligo Quay.

The Free State government offered compensation to the railways to pay for the destruction. The most notable consequence on the SLNCR was the purchasing of three bogie passenger coaches in place of the eight 6-wheelers destroyed. These were the only bogie passenger coaches on the line, and although ordered as late as 1924, they had clerestory roofs. Carrignagat Junction signal box was replaced by a temporary six-lever frame in a hut. This had to suffice until the junction was taken out of use on 7th September 1930, from which time parallel single-line working was introduced between the site of the junction and Ballysodare station.

1921 saw the SLNCR take tender engines into its stock for the first time, with two 4-4-0s acquired from the GNR replacing the two original 0-6-2Ts of 1877. However, the haulage capability of these 4-4-0s proved inadequate and, after seven and ten years respectively, they were replaced by a series of 0-6-0s, also acquired from the Great Northern. The last of these was withdrawn in 1949, although the hire of another 0-6-0 from the Great Northern was resorted to for a short period of time during 1950/1.

In due course the border between the two parts of Ireland was to have significant effects upon the established patterns of trade which the lines which now found themselves straddling the frontier, like the SLNCR, had been built to support. Perhaps the most important initial effect of the new political order on the railway was that, although most of the line was in the Irish Free State, because the eastern end of it entered Northern Ireland, it could not be forced to amalgamate with the other lines which were wholly within the southern jurisdiction which were grouped in 1925 to form the Great Southern Railways. Following the Second World War the SLNCR's cross border route also kept it out of the hands of the Ulster Transport Authority, the organisation set up to nationalise the railways of Northern Ireland. Because of its geographical situation, the SLNCR was able to maintain its independence throughout its existence.

Customs posts were set up in 1923. H M Customs established themselves at Belcoo and their Free State counterparts opened for business at Glenfarne. There were also Customs offices at Enniskillen and Manorhamilton. Traffic from the Free State counties to Dublin inevitably drifted towards the former MGWR route and away from the SLNCR/GNR lines through Northern Ireland, although in 1927 the SLNCR entered into a bond permitting imports for Northern Ireland via the port of Sligo to pass through the Irish Free State under seal, and from 1936 Free State to Free State traffic could pass through Northern Ireland in sealed vans or containers. The effects of the border on trade were severe. A multitude of different duties and tariffs were levied on goods, trains were delayed whilst customs examinations were carried out, passengers had to have their luggage checked by sometimes over zealous officials on both sides of the border and smuggling became a major industry in the border counties. All of this occurred at a time when the competition from the roads began to affect the railways significantly for the first time.

Economies, Innovation and Subsidies

A 12-week strike by railway staff throughout Northern Ireland in early 1933 severely disrupted services on the SLNCR, and when the strike was over, not only were passenger services reduced from three to two in each direction each day, but a through competing bus service had been established between Enniskillen and Sligo. Freight traffic additionally suffered from the so called 'Economic War' between the Free State and Great Britain. This resulted from the Free State withholding from late in 1932, land annuities due to the British government. In retaliation a tax was imposed by Britain on, inter alia, imports of Irish cattle, a staple traffic on the SLNCR.

The financial results for August 1933 were significant. Receipts were down by £564 compared with a year previously and expenditure exceeded receipts by £685. However, in 1935

the Northern Ireland government started to subsidise the railway, on the grounds that its difficulties largely stemmed from the trade dispute with the Irish Free State. This 'Grant-in-Aid', as it was known, compensated the SLNCR each year for its operating loss.

Exploration of cheaper methods of operation was given added impetus by the financial situation in the wake of the 1933 strike. In 1932 the company had tried over its line one of the the GNR's new diesel railcars, and had been pleased with how much cheaper it was to run than a steam train, how it had negotiated the difficult route, and how it could readily call at level crossings to pick up and set down passengers. By the time the SLNCR decided, in the summer of 1934, to purchase a light self-propelled vehicle, the GNR was also experimenting with a road bus converted to run on rails. A Great Northern bus was therefore bought by the company and was converted at the GNR works at Dundalk into a railbus. The railbus was delivered on 20th June 1935. With the railbus came a four-wheel luggage trailer. Passenger services were immediately restored to their pre-strike level by the use of the railbus. A second railbus was acquired by the company in 1938.

Although the 'Economic War' was resolved in 1938, the Northern Ireland government continued to subsidise the SLNCR. Indeed, during the Second World War, known as 'The Emergency' in neutral Ireland, when petrol was scarce and much traffic that had earlier left the railways returned, the SLNCR registered a profit for five separate years, though it still received Grant-in Aid from the Northern government. The railways themselves did not escape wartime fuel shortages, the SLNCR was sometimes down to as little as two weeks supply of steam coal during these years. Things were much worse in the neutral south. The SLNCR/GNR route from Sligo to Dublin benefited when on occasions the GSR was unable to run any trains over their direct route, a situation which even applied as late as 1947.

It was during the 1939-45 period that the Sligo, Leitrim & Northern Counties Railway first ventured into an advertised road freight service, though this was confined to the Irish side of the border. This service started in 1943 when two lorries were purchased, although it should be mentioned that the company had been running a purely local delivery service since 1934 from Belcoo station to the village of Blacklion, just across the border in County Cavan. Then in 1945, the company took over the Blacklion to Manorhamilton and Sligo bus service, involving the purchase of two buses. The company's bus network was later expanded by the addition of other routes.

The other notable step forward in the 1939 to 1945 period was the ordering of a modern duo-directional railcar from Messrs. Walkers of Wigan. This was ordered in 1944 though the railcar was not delivered until 9th July 1947, by which time the estimated cost of £8,000 had risen to £10,522.

The Final Years

With the ending of the Second World War in 1945, petrol eventually became more freely available and road transport regained and expanded its ground taking away from the railway traffic which had temporarily returned during the war. On the SLNCR a serious locomotive situation added to the problems and as no suitable locomotives were available for hire from the GNR or Coras Iompair Eireann, the post-1945 successor of the GSR in the south, approaches were made to Beyer Peacock about ordering two more 0-6-4 tanks. These, the 'Lough' class, were completed in 1949, but were not taken into stock until 1951 because of problems in paying for them. In the end, a hire purchase arrangement was agreed, in 1950, with two thirds of the initial payment of £3,000 being contributed by the Northern Ireland government.

The company's final post-war financial difficulties, stemming from the loss of traffic to the roads, alluded to already, were compounded by elements such as demands for higher pay, equal to or related to that received by staff on other railways in Ireland. On top of this, in 1946 the Northern government reduced its Grant-in-Aid to £1,500 per annum, this was in a year when the company reported an operating loss of £2,831. Some easement was secured from the Great Northern Railway in 1950 when they increased by £2,000 each half-year the proportion of through traffic receipts allowed to the SLNCR, although before long the GNR was itself in trouble, threatening closure of its system in 1951. Two years later the GNR was taken over by a Board representing the governments of the Republic of Ireland and Northern Ireland. So serious became the SLNCR's problems, that moves to wind up the company received unanimous support at its general meeting early in 1952. Pressure on the two governments secured, shortly afterwards, a subsidy of £3,500 per annum from Dublin, followed by a raising to £3,000 of the Grant-in-Aid from the northern government.

In May 1955, however, with a working loss the previous year of £10,534, the Northern Ireland government announced that its Grant-in-Aid for that year would be its last. The Dublin authorities offered an increase in their subsidy to £8,500 if Belfast would reciprocate, but this went unheeded and SLNCR staff were given notice as from 11th June 1955, employment thereafter being on a daily basis, the intention being to close the railway on 1st January 1956. This crisis was averted by pressure, once again, from many interests, resulting in a £10,000 subsidy from the Republic of Ireland for 1956, provided that the West of Ireland Cattle Traders' Association paid a levy on each wagon of cattle forwarded over the line, which they did.

By then, however, the Northern Ireland government had signalled its intention to close the Great Northern line through Enniskillen, thus threatening to rupture the SLNCR's slender lifeline. The company, along with many bodies including the government of the Republic of Ireland and the Great Northern Railway Board itself, strongly protested at the proposed closure of the GNR lines. The Republic could, incidentally, under the legislation setting up the GNR board, have averted the closures provided it sustained fully the financial losses, but this, perhaps understandably, the Dublin authorities were not prepared to do. Dublin did, nevertheless, promise a subsidy of £15,000 to the SLNCR for 1957, but in July the government of the Republic indicated that the

Setting off from Florencecourt down an initial 1 in 66 gradient is the 7.20pm mixed from Enniskillen to Sligo on 2nd June 1954, with *Lough Erne* hauling coach No 9, several wagons and a brake van. This picture, and another by the author depicting railcar B approaching Belcoo from the Sligo direction, appeared on the outside front cover of the SLNCR's final timetable booklet valid from 25th June 1957 'until further notice' – which turned out to be the closure of the line on 30th September that year (see page 79). It will be noted that the up home signal, at the rear of the train, has an arm with twin, red and green spectacles, unlike the single spectacle arms at this station which are illustrated on page 28. Author

subsidy would be discontinued after 30th September 1957, when the GNR line through Enniskillen was to close. As late as September 1957 various proposals were put to the Northern government by outside interests to try to avert closure of the Great Northern and SLNCR lines. The southern government indicated its preparedness to continue its £15,000 annual subvention to the SLNCR if a rail outlet at Enniskillen was available. This proposal was put in vain to the Stormont government as late as 18th September. So it was only on 20th September that the SLNCR decided to discontinue its rail and road services after the last journeys on Monday, 30th September 1957. This time there was no reprieve and the services did indeed cease and the Sligo, Leitrim & Northern Counties Railway reached the end of the line as did the Great Northern route through Enniskillen.

Perhaps, on reflection, it is remarkable that the SLNCR survived for so long amid its almost perpetual financial problems before being finally submerged by them. Furthermore, it is ironic that it was the closure of a section of the Great Northern Railway, always the more powerful and prosperous, almost paternal, neighbour, that eventually precipitated the SLNCR's demise.

Post Mortem

Various train movements took place during the first five days of October 1957 to clear 'foreign'

wagons from the line, to deploy SLNCR locomotives and rolling stock to agreed holding points at Enniskillen, Manorhamilton and Collooney, to enable officers and staff to see to various matters connected with the line's closure and finally, on Saturday 5th October 1957, to take the last pay to staff at stations.

A new company, the Sligo, Leitrim and Northern Counties Railway Company Limited was registered in Northern Ireland on 17th December 1957, to attend to the winding up and disposal of assets. The last meeting of the original SLNCR company took place on 14th January 1958 when it was recorded in the Minute Books that ten members of staff were still employed at that time. The company's property and rolling stock was prepared for disposal by auction, the auctions taking place at Enniskillen in October 1958 for property and equipment in Northern Ireland and at Manorhamilton in April 1959 to dispose of moveable or removable property in the Republic of Ireland. Fixed property such as station houses in the Republic were finally auctioned off in November 1959. The most notable survivors of the sell-off were the Walker built railcar, railcar B, which was purchased by CIE, and the last two 0-6-4Ts which were bought, not from the SLNCR, but from their owners, Beyer Peacock, by the Ulster Transport Authority. Railcar B and one of the 0-6-4Ts, *Lough Erne*, have subsequently been preserved.

AUTHOR'S NOTE

I first set my eyes on the Sligo, Leitrim & Northern Counties Railway one evening in May 1952 during a week long tour of the Great Northern Railway. On arrival at Enniskillen, there was the renowned 7.20pm mixed train to Sligo waiting to leave.

Here at last was that, to me, distant railway which was of the Irish standard 5ft 3in gauge and still privately owned, whose locomotives were all of the unusual 0-6-4T wheel arrangement, and which were known only by name, never by numbers. One of the two latest 'Lough' class 0-6-4Ts, less than twelve months in service, hauled the 7.20pm that evening.

A year later I made the first of six visits to explore the SLNCR, although the evening I chose for my first ride on the line on the 7.20pm as far as Manorhamilton, was one of those on which the steam mixed train was replaced by a railbus!

In 1962, five years after the closure of the SLNCR, I gave a talk on the line to the London area of the Irish Railway Record Society. In view of the information which I had gathered and the desire on the part of the Society's London area to venture into book publishing, I was asked to enlarge my research to produce a full history of the line in book form. After help from other members, notably Bob Clements, Peter Rowledge and John Smith, the book was published in 1970. A further edition, with a few amendments and additions, came out in 1981, this time to help raise funds for the Railway Preservation Society of Ireland's overhaul of the preserved SLNCR 0-6-4T, *Lough Erne*.

In the publishing field, the SLNCR came back into focus in 1997 when Michael Hamilton wrote *Down Memory Line*, (Drumlin Publications), which related his experiences of growing up alongside the line in one of the level crossing gatehouses, and then working on the railway. He was a guard at the time of the line's closure. His book is a most interesting social and transport history.

And so to this present book. I was persuaded, after some initial reluctance on my part, by Midland Publishing that a volume on the SLNCR would make an appropriate addition to their *Irish Railway Pictorial* series. In the selection of the almost two hundred photographs which make up this book, I have tried to offer a broader view of the railway. I have included not just the trains, but stations, signals, structures, buses, documents, timetables and other printed materials produced by the company. In addition there are photographs of some of the staff who ran the railway, for in truth nothing would have happened without them.

Photographs of this delightful railway do not appear that frequently. I hope this collection will serve to evoke pleasant memories for those who remember the line and perhaps show later generations, who were not fortunate enough to experience the SLNCR for themselves, why this impoverished system in a remote part of Ireland, has had such an enduring appeal down through the decades.

The many photographers whose work has made this book possible are acknowledged individually in the captions. I acknowledge here collectively, their support for this project, with sincere thanks.

In conclusion, I owe a considerable debt of gratitude to my wife, who has patiently endured my relapse into thoughts of the SLNCR during the time it has taken me to prepare this book for publication. Apart from her general forbearance, she has also greatly assisted me in reading the proofs. This is not an attempt to excuse myself from any remaining errors, which despite her best efforts, are my responsibility.

Neil Sprinks
Dinas Powys, Vale of Glamorgan
January 2001

In the SLNCR's later years, most passenger services were operated by railbus or railcar. This picture shows the second railbus A, in its rebodied form, and its trailer, approaching Enniskillen with the 6.20am service from Sligo on 2nd June 1954. To the right of this picture is the down GNR starting signal controlling SLNCR departures towards Sligo. Author

LOCOMOTIVES

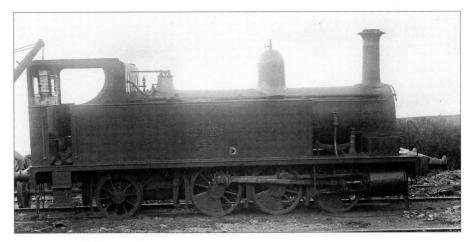

Right: The SLNCR's first locomotives were two Avonside built 0-6-2Ts *Pioneer* (works number 1197) and *Sligo* (works number 1198), built in 1877 and delivered to Enniskillen in December initially for use on construction work. This 1902 photograph shows *Sligo*. The locomotives were reported as unsteady and slow. Their driving wheels had a diameter of 3ft 9½in and their original boilers worked at a pressure of 130 lbs per sq inch.

Below: In 1882 came the first of the SLNCR's renowned Beyer Peacock 0-6-4Ts. In this first class were five locomotives, *Fermanagh* and *Leitrim* (1882), *Lurganboy* (1895) and *Lissadell* and *Hazlewood* (1899). The diameter of their driving wheels was 4ft 9ins. This 1902 photograph shows *Lissadell* (works No.4073) in its original form. The copper capped chimneys and Salter safety valves disappeared in subsequent reboilerings. The capacity of the coal bunker was later increased by the fitting of coal rails. *Lissadell*, named after the home, north-west of Sligo, of the Gore-Booth family who were amongst the principal promoters of the line, was withdrawn in 1954, although it remained at Manorhamilton until after the line's closure. The locomotives started life in a lined olive green livery with polished domes and chimney caps, before the plain black became standard.
Both H Fayle, author's collection

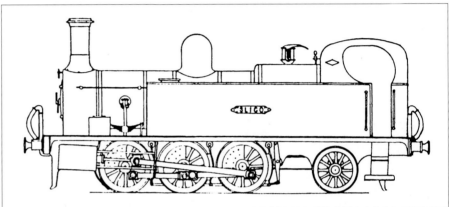

Above: Eventually the 0-6-2Ts *Pioneer* and *Sligo* were rebuilt with Belpaire boilers giving them an increased pressure of 150 lbs per sq inch. A more spacious cab with improved protection for the crew was also fitted. This drawing, by J F McEwan, reproduced by courtesy of the Stephenson Locomotive Society, shows *Sligo* in this form. *Pioneer* was rebuilt in 1907, *Sligo* the following year. Both locomotives were withdrawn in 1921 and sold for scrap seven years later.

Left: 4-4-0T *Erne*, built by Hudswell Clarke (works No 261) was a passenger locomotive built in 1883 with 5ft driving wheels. As early as January 1884 it was derailed near Enniskillen, indicative of a generally problematic locomotive which many crews were afraid to take out on the road. Author's collection

Centre: In 1884-85 *Erne* was rebuilt as a 4-4-2T, the frames being lengthened for this purpose, although the coal bunker was not enlarged. The locomotive continued to be a source of trouble, however, and appears not to have been used if another engine was available. In June 1911 it was decided to withdraw *Erne* from service, and within a year it had been sold for scrap and broken up at Manorhamilton. H Fayle, author's collection

Below left: In 1898 the SLNCR purchased from the engineering contractors Fisher and Lefanu the Hunslet 0-4-0T, *Faugh a Ballagh* (works No 178 of 1878). It remained on the company's books, in use for banking duties and ballast trains, until sold in October 1905 to contractor Robert Worthington for use on the building of the Castleblaney, Keady and Armagh line. *Faugh a Ballagh* was no stranger to the SLNCR, having started life in the ownership of Arthur Tottenham, a former SLNCR Chairman and in 1878 one of the contractors building the line. *Faugh a Ballagh* was delivered to Enniskillen on 23rd March 1878 and taken later by road for use in the company's ballast quarry at Belcoo. After the line was completed in 1882, Tottenham and his brother Henry who was both Permanent Way and Locomotive Superintendent allowed the SLNCR to use the locomotive until Henry left the company's service in 1892 selling *Faugh a Ballagh* to the aforementioned Fisher and Lefanu for use on building the Claremorris and Collooney line. The locomotive's name is an old Irish war cry meaning 'Clear the way'. Standing by *Faugh a Ballagh* in this 1902 photograph is Stephen Murphy, SLNCR Engineer and Locomotive Superintendent, from 1892 to 1911. H Fayle, author's collection

Opposite page top: 0-6-0T *Waterford* also came to the SLNCR from Fisher and Lefanu after use on the construction of the Claremorris to Collooney line. It was built in 1893 by Hunslet (works No 591) and purchased by the SLNCR in 1899. Seen here in 1902, it was used mostly for shunting and banking at Collooney from where up trains faced a climb to a summit at Ballintogher, which included sections at 1 in 50. *Waterford* was reboilered in 1915, eventually being sold for scrap in 1928 along with the original 0-6-2Ts, *Pioneer* and *Sligo*. H Fayle, author's collection

Centre: **Two Beyer Peacock 4-4-0 tender locomotives were purchased second-hand from the GNR in 1921 to replace the 0-6-2Ts. The 4-4-0s proved unsatisfactory because of their limited haulage capacity. They were named by the SLNCR** *Blacklion,* **after the County Cavan village served from Belcoo station, and** *Glencar,* **after a lough in County Sligo. Both went to the GNR's Dundalk works in June 1928 where** *Blacklion* **received the boiler and tender of** *Glencar.* **This photograph shows** *Blacklion* **in this condition at Sligo in 1929, two years before it was withdrawn, though it was not sold for scrap until 1938. In 1933 its tender was converted to a weed spraying vehicle.** *Blacklion* **had originally been built in 1885 (works No 2516), its GNR number 118, is still just visible on the loco's cabside in this picture.** *Glencar,* **the former GNR No 119, was withdrawn in 1928.** H C Casserley

Below: **To replace the 4-4-0s, two Beyer Peacock-built A class 0-6-0 tender locomotives were bought from the GNR. One, named** *Glencar* **by the SLNCR arrived in 1928, the other named** *Sligo,* **in 1931.** *Sligo* **was returned to the GNR in 1940 and replaced by another 0-6-0 of the same class, which also took that name. Other 0-6-0s were occasionally hired from the GNR to make up for a temporary locomotive shortage. This photo shows the second** *Sligo* **at Collooney in May 1947. Built in 1882 (works No 2116), at the time of its sale to the SLNCR, it bore the GNR number 69. This engine was withdrawn and sold for scrap in 1949.** John Dewing

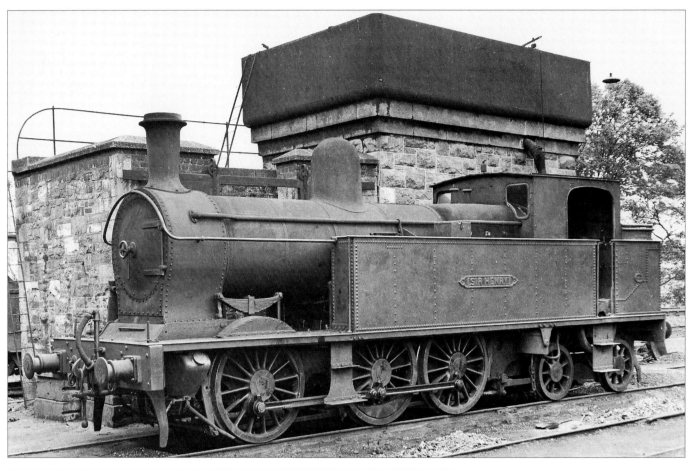

Top: **A new and enlarged series of Beyer Peacock 0-6-4Ts entered service from 1904, comprising three locomotives, *Sir Henry* (1904), *Enniskillen* (1905) and *Lough Gill* (1917). They became known as the 'Large Tanks', the 1882-1899 series of 0-6-4Ts becoming the 'Small Tanks'. The driving wheel diameter of the new machines was 4ft 8ins, one inch less than on the 'Small Tanks'. New boilers were fitted in 1929, 1931 and 1939 respectively and all three locomotives remained in the company's stock until closure in 1957. This picture shows *Sir Henry* (works No 4592), at Sligo shed on 29th July 1956. The locomotive's name honours Sir Henry Gore-Booth, a Chairman of the SLNCR whose home at Lissadell was commemorated in the name of one of the 'Small Tanks'.** Author

Above: **The final additions to the SLNCR fleet were two Beyer Peacock 0-6-4Ts, similar to the *'Sir Henry'* class or 'Large Tanks', but with a new type of cab, extended bunker, shorter chimney and dome and enlarged cylinders. They were named *Lough Melvin* and *Lough Erne* after lakes in the counties of Leitrim and Fermanagh respectively. Although completed in 1949, they did not enter** service until the summer of 1951. The intervening time was occupied by the negotiations, referred to in the introduction, whereby the locomotives remained the property of Beyer Peacock, but were used by the SLNCR under a hire-purchase arrangement. This picture shows *Lough Erne*, in undercoat, standing in the yard of Beyer Peacock's Manchester works in 1949 shortly after the locomotive was completed. After closure of the line, *Lough Erne* (works No 7242) was sold by Beyer Peacock in 1959 to the UTA, who numbered it 27. When finally withdrawn it was bought for preservation in 1970 and is in the care of the Railway Preservation Society of Ireland at their Whitehead depot. The two 1949 tanks were the last conventional steam locomotives supplied to an Irish railway operator. Robert Fysh

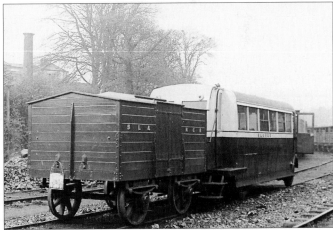

RAILBUSES AND RAILCAR

Top: **The first railbus, denoted A, was an ex-GNR AEC vehicle converted to run on rails by the GNR at Dundalk works. It was delivered to the SLNCR, along with a four wheel luggage trailer with a tarpaulin cover, on 20th June 1935. Alterations to the bus included it being equipped with Howden-Meredith patent wheels, steel flanged rims around pneumatic tyres, and the fitting of doors, platforms and steps on** both sides at the rear. Seating capacity was 32. Initially the railbus had a 6-cylinder 40hp petrol engine. After trials with a GNR diesel railbus in 1936, a diesel engine was fitted to railbus A early in 1938. This view shows A and its trailer at Manorhamilton on 29th June 1938. Railbus A was broken up following a collision with a steam locomotive at Glenfarne on 7th March 1939. H C Casserley

Above left: **The second railbus, 2A, pictured here at Enniskillen on 29th June 1939, arrived the previous year. It also was a converted GNR AEC road bus but with a** completely new body for rail use and a new diesel engine. 2A acquired the luggage trailer from A after the latter was withdrawn in March 1939. 2A and the trailer remained in service until the SLNCR closed. Robert Fysh collection

Above right: **The luggage trailer was later rebuilt. Its sides were raised and the tarpaulin was replaced by a solid, slightly pitched roof with hinged openings, as seen in this photo taken at Enniskillen on 21st April 1948. H C Casserley**

Above: **As the timetable required two railbuses and they were so economical to operate, the loss of A in March 1939 could not be tolerated for long and a replacement was obtained later that year in the form of the prototype GNR railbus D, latterly D1, which itself had been a road bus until converted for rail use in 1934. Before delivery to the SLNCR it was given the diesel engine from the withdrawn railbus A, whose identity it also assumed, becoming the company's second railbus A. It is shown here with a luggage trailer, at Enniskillen on 31st August 1950. The railbus had folding doors and steps each side behind the driver's cab, instead of the usual railbus rear swing doors, steps and platforms.** John Dewing

Above: **In December 1950 the second railbus A went back to Dundalk works where the GNR fitted a fresh second-hand body from a GNR road bus, converted for rail use with rear platforms and doors. In this photograph, the rebuilt railbus A** is on the turntable at Enniskillen. The similarity between the rebodied A and railbus 2A will be noted. Railbus A and its luggage trailer, remained on the line until closure in 1957. **Charles Friel collection**

Right: **The SLNCR's most modern vehicle was diesel railcar B, built by Walker Brothers of Wigan. Delivered to Enniskillen in July 1947 it is photographed here at Sligo in August of the following year. A power unit and driving cab mounted on a four-wheel bogie with outside connecting rods was articulated with a 59-seat passenger section carried on a normal bogie. A driving position in a half-cab at the outer end of the passenger saloon avoided the need to turn the vehicle, as was necessary with the railbuses, at each end of a journey. The passenger saloon and adjacent parcels compartment had sliding doors. A box-type protrusion on the roof of the driving cab, encasing the cooling apparatus, was occasionally fitted as shown in some subsequent photographs.**
After the closure of the SLNCR in 1957, railcar B was bought by CIE who numbered it 2509. On the SLNCR, railcar B and the railbuses ran in a two tone green livery with white roofs. Michael Hamilton has identified three of the people in this photograph, Guard Martin Brannigan (outer left), Driver Paddy McTernan (inner left) and Fireman Michael Harte (outer right). Railcar B's usual driver was Paddy Nevin, which led to the vehicle being sometimes known as 'Paddy Nevin's railcar'. John Gillham

Below: **This photograph, taken at Enniskillen on 29th May 1957, shows the 2-ton luggage trailer of the second railbus A. The trailer, ordered in 1942, comprised a body built at Manorhamilton, and fitted** there to the bogie frame and wheels from a GSR Sentinel steam railcar. This picture also illustrates well the rear doors, platform and steps of the railbus itself. F W Shuttleworth

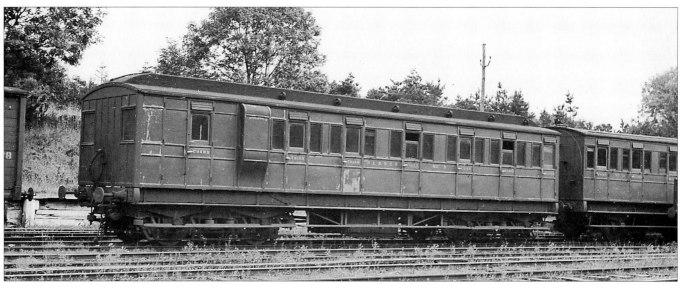

TRI-COMPOSITE COACHES

Top: **Before exploring the SLNCR, it is worth looking at the three 44ft 6in long tri-composite clerestory bogie coaches ordered from Hurst Nelson in 1924 to replace vehicles lost in the 'Troubles'. Although perhaps anachronisms even when built, these coaches were nevertheless the SLNCR's latest locomotive hauled passenger vehicles and therefore feature in many of the photographs that follow. This is particularly true of the 1950s when many of our pictures were taken. At that time the only advertised steam hauled passenger carrying service was the 7.20pm 'Mixed' from Enniskillen to Sligo. On this train passenger accommodation was usually provided by coach No 9, all other passenger services being worked by the railbuses or railcar B. Pictured here at Enniskillen on 31st August 1950, No 9, alone of the three coaches, had a brake compartment. In order from the**

brake compartment (nearest the camera), were two Third class compartments, a First, another Third, a Second and then a Second class coupe with end windows similar to those visible at the brake compartment end. All three coaches remained in stock until the SLNCR closed.
E E Smith, John Dewing collection

Above: **The other two coaches, Nos 10 and 11, shared the same layout. From the end nearest the camera in this view of No 10 taken at Sligo station on 30th June 1950, the order was Second class coupe, Second class, Third class saloon, First class and two Third class compartments. No 10 did differ from No 11 in not having any lighting, being intended for regular use on the 10.20am Sligo to Enniskillen and 1.40pm return trains of the pre-railbus era. These trains usually hauled in the 1920s by one of the 4-4-0s and known as the 'Mail trains', being passenger only when other services were mixed, made good connections with the cross channel steamers via Belfast and Dublin. From 1931 all three coaches were equipped with steam heating. Second class**

compartments in all SLNCR coaches were reclassified as Thirds when Second class was discontinued on the SLNCR from 1st January 1951. Later, on 3rd June 1956, when European railways went over to a two class system, all Third class compartments became Second class, as on other Irish and British lines. Examination of this and the previous photograph reveals that compartment doors were hung on the right, with handles and locks on the left, when viewed from outside. This was a peculiarity of all coaches built for the SLNCR and was opposite to the general practice in the British Isles. SLNCR carriage livery was unlined maroon. John Edgington

Below: **The single First class compartment, this view is of the interior of No 9, in all three bogie coaches was divided by this central sliding door into smoking and non-smoking sections.** Desmond Coakham

ENNISKILLEN STATION

Below: Enniskillen was the the most important station on the SLNCR where the line made its vital link with the GNR which gave it access to the ports of Derry, Belfast, Greenore and Dublin. Here too were located the line's General and Traffic Managers. From 1883 SLNCR passenger trains used a bay platform at the Dundalk end of the GNR station where 'Small Tank' 0-6-4T *Lurganboy* and tri-composite 6-wheel coach No 12 are seen on 29th June 1950 with the 7.20pm mixed to Sligo, to which goods wagons and a brake van will be attached in the SLNCR yard outside the station before heading west. In the dock alongside the bay is cattle wagon No 29. *Lurganboy* was built by Beyer Peacock (works No 3677) in 1895 and remained in traffic until 1953 when it was sold for scrap and broken up. John Edgington

Bottom: **This picture gives a wider view of the SLNCR passenger bay and the adjacent dock with its loading gauge. In the bay is the second, rebodied, railbus A and trailer, waiting to depart as the 1.50pm to Sligo on 31st May 1954. Behind railbus A is coach No.9, stabled for use on the 7.20pm mixed to Sligo later in the day (see the caption to the timetable bill on page 76 for a description of this working). Author**

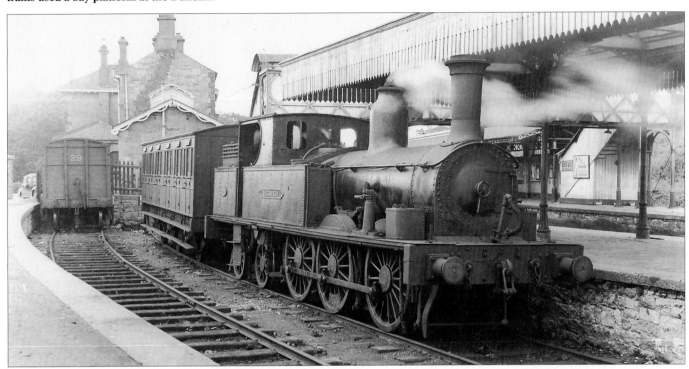

Top: 'Small Tank' *Hazlewood* stands in the bay at the head of the 7.20pm mixed to Sligo, on 24th May 1955, with bogie clerestory coach No 11 providing the passenger accommodation. Once again thanks to Michael Hamilton for identifying the members of staff in the picture who are, from left to right, Porter John Howe,

Foreman Jimmy McHugh, Fireman Bertie Hegarty and Driver Tommie Marren. *Hazlewood*, the last of the 1882-1899 series of Beyer Peacock 0-6-4Ts, was completed in 1899 (works No 4074). Named after the home of one of the SLNCR's promoters, Owen Wynne, it remained in traffic until closure. Author

Above: Railcar B in the bay platform on 4th September 1957, waiting to depart as the 12 noon summer only service to Sligo. Behind, just visible, is railbus 2A which will form the 1.45pm service. The non-motor end of the railcar is shown. The window on the right beside the cab, gave passengers a good view along the line. Keith Walton

Above: **'Large Tank' 0-6-4T** *Enniskillen* **is in the down GNR platform at Enniskillen on a wagon transfer working on 22nd August 1957. On the right is GNR PP class 4-4-0 No 44 in the GNR shed yard. Just visible on the left is SLNCR railbus 2A and its trailer signalled to depart, presumably as the 1.45pm service to Sligo.** *Enniskillen*, **probably named after the Earl of Enniskillen, one of the SLNCR's promoters, was the second 'Large Tank', being completed by Beyer Peacock (works No 4720), in 1905. It remained in traffic until the line's closure.** A E Bennett

Below left: **In this view the train in the bay platform, formed of a GNR luggage van and one of the SLNCR's bogie coaches, Nos 10 or 11, is headed by 0-6-0** *Glencar*. **This locomotive, built for the Great Northern by Beyer Peacock in 1890 (works No 3273), carried the number 31 on the GNR. It was purchased by the SLNCR in 1928 and remained on the line until 1949 when it was withdrawn and sold for scrap.** John Langford collection

Below right: **On 20th April 1948, 'Small Tank'** *Hazlewood* **stands with the 7.30pm to Sligo at the dock platform instead of the usual bay platform.** H C Casserley

Above: **In this photograph of 24th May 1955, we see the junction of the SLNCR with the GNR, formed of a single track from the SLNCR yard leading to the down GNR line. The leading wheels of GNR U class 4-4-0 No 198** *Lough Swilly*, **arriving on a train from Dundalk and Clones, are just at the point where the two lines converge. All movements over the connecting line required a shunt move from or to the main SLNCR line which, coming out of the bay in the GNR station (the track in the centre foreground), curves away through the SLNCR yard.**

On the farthest SLNCR track, against which is the platform with the SLNCR offices, is one of the 'Large Tanks', already turned after its arrival from Sligo. To the right of the train is the GNR's Enniskillen South signal box which controlled the junction. No 198's sister locomotive, No 197 *Lough Neagh*, completes the picture. Author

Below: **This picture, taken on 15th June 1957, shows from across the GNR tracks, 'Large Tank'** *Sir Henry* **with coach No 9, which had recently been repainted with** gold-shaded First and Second on its doors, preparing the 7.20pm mixed to Sligo. Behind *Sir Henry* is the SLNCR goods shed and between the locomotive and GNR PG class 0-6-0 No 151 on the GNR shed is another view of the curving SLNCR yard through which passed the main running line to Sligo. In the vicinity of this yard was the SLNCR's temporary platform and terminus which was used from the opening of the line in 1879 until the GNR station was enlarged and could accommodate SLNCR trains from 1883. Michael Davies

Photographs on the opposite page:

Top: **Taken from the dock, this view shows the second railbus A in its original form. It has just arrived from Sligo on 18th May 1950. This view showing the near side of the vehicle may be compared with the offside view given on page 12.**
H C Casserley

Bottom:**This wider panorama from the same vantage point shows railbus 2A and trailer after arrival from Sligo on 25th September 1953. To the left of the picture is the GNR locomotive shed and yard, in the right background the SLNCR yard can be seen, curving alongside the SLNCR line to Sligo, where one of the company's locomotives is shunting.** R K McKenny

Above: 'Small Tank' *Lurganboy* stands alongside the SLNCR office platform on 31st August 1950. The 6-wheel passenger coach is No 2, a four-compartment composite purchased from the GNR in 1926. Two outer Second class compartments flanked two centre First class compartments. The vehicle was 27ft long, it had steam heating and electric lighting and unlike *Lurganboy*, survived until closure. This locomotive was named after the home, near Manorhamilton, of Mr R E Davis, one of the line's promoters, who was appointed Secretary to the company, leading to Lurganboy being the registered office of the SLNCR throughout its existence. From 1890 to 1897, when the line was in financial difficulties, Mr Davis was Manager and Receiver as well.
John Dewing

Above: 0-6-4T *Lough Melvin* (works No 7138 of 1949) is seen here after arrival with the 6.30am 'Livestock and Goods' train from Sligo on 31st May 1954, prior to shunting wagons on to the sidings which had access to the GNR. The shunting has already started, a cut in the train has been made behind the ninth wagon.

The GNR locomotive shed and the line from Dundalk and Clones are on the left. After the SLNCR's closure, *Lough Melvin* was sold by Beyer Peacock to the UTA in 1959, who numbered it 26. *Lough Melvin* was withdrawn by the UTA in 1965 and sold for scrap in 1968. Author

Right: **Standing on the crossover leading to the track alongside the SLNCR office platform on 22nd August 1947, is GNR E class 0-6-0 No 193 during a nine-month period of loan to the SLNCR. No 193 was one of the last locomotives built for the Irish North Western Railway to remain in traffic. It had also been on the SLNCR in 1928 for trials when the use of 0-6-0's on the line was first considered.** Charles Friel collection

Centre: **One of the first two of the 0-6-4T 'Small Tanks', *Leitrim*, stands in the SLNCR yard on 29th July 1936. *Leitrim* (Beyer Peacock works No 2138) and sister locomotive *Fermanagh* dated from 1882. In 1947 this engine was the first 0-6-4 tank to be withdrawn. After various parts were removed for spares, *Leitrim* was sold for scrap in 1952.** Jim Jarvis

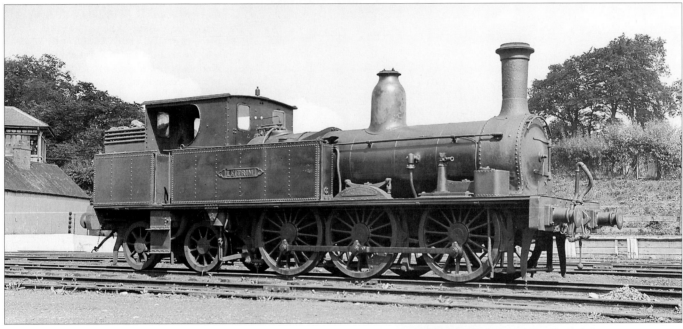

Right: **Ex-GNR 0-6-0 *Sligo* stands in Enniskillen Yard on 24th June 1937. This locomotive was the first of two 0-6-0s to bear this name. Having been bought from the GNR in 1931, it was returned to them in 1940 to be replaced by an identical locomotive in better condition which took the same name. The locomotive shown here was Beyer Peacock works No 3274 of 1890 and was numbered 149 by the GNR.** H C Casserley

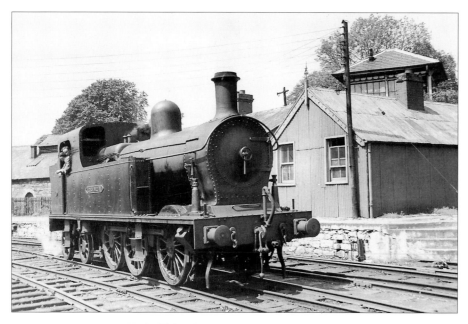

Left: **This further photograph of** *Lough Melvin* **at Enniskillen on 31st May 1954 shows the locomotive after turning, ready for its return journey to Sligo on the 2.15pm goods train. To the right of the locomotive is more detail of the SLNCR offices housing the General and Traffic Managers and their staff.** Author

Centre: **Twelve days previously, on 19th May 1954,** *Lough Melvin* **was on the 7.20pm mixed to Sligo, shown here leaving Enniskillen. The station is in the background with the canopy over the SLNCR bay platform discernable above the brake van. On the right is the outer end of the GNR locomotive shed, and separated from it by the GNR line to Dundalk and Clones, is the platform on which the SLNCR offices stood. At the near end of this platform, the well of the SLNCR's turntable may be seen. Above the coach, bogie brake composite No 9, can be seen the SLNCR goods shed and to the right above the leading cattle wagon is the company's water tank. To the right of the brake van at the far end of the office platform is the track linking the Sligo line to the GNR system.** S C Nash

Below: **On the up side (on this line up meant in the direction of Enniskillen), on the approach to the station, two lines in the SLNCR yard each terminated in a locomotive shed. Railcar B is standing outside the larger of these in this view taken on 29th May 1957. On this occasion the protective hood sometimes fitted around the cooling apparatus on the roof of the driving cab, is in position. In the smaller shed, on the left, is railbus 2A, with its trailer outside. The line to Sligo is on the far left, with the parapet of the bridge over the Tempo road just visible.** F W Shuttleworth

ON THE OUTSKIRTS OF ENNISKILLEN

Right: **The rear of the 7.20pm mixed to Sligo is on the bridge over the Tempo road in this picture of the train leaving Enniskillen on 2nd May 1950 behind 'Small Tank'** *Lissadell.* **Above the six-wheel tri-composite coach No 12 built by Ashbury in 1899, is the GNR signal controlling up trains on the approach to Enniskillen yard and station.** Robert Fysh

Bottom: **0-6-4T** *Lough Melvin* **with the 6.30am 'Livestock and Goods' from Sligo is shown here, on 2nd June 1954, passing through the Castlecoole woods on the approach to Enniskillen.** Author

Above: **About one mile from Enniskillen was the 467ft. bridge of lattice girder spans, supported on masonry abutments and four pairs of cast iron pillars, which carried the line over the River Erne. Known commonly as the Killyhevlin or Weir's Bridge, officially as structure No 4, the maximum permitted axle loading over the bridge was 13 tons. A speed limit of 5mph** applied and double heading was not allowed. In this picture, taken on 17th June 1952, *Lough Melvin* crosses the bridge with the 9.45am goods from Sligo to Enniskillen. J J Smith

Top left: **Weir's Bridge from the Enniskillen end, viewed from a train on 15th August 1957.** A E Bennett

Top right: **Railcar B eases its way across the Weir's Bridge on 25th May 1955, operating the 4.00pm Sligo to Enniskillen service.** Author

BETWEEN ENNISKILLEN & FLORENCECOURT

Below: This delightful picture of the 7.20pm mixed from Enniskillen to Sligo on 8th August 1956 introduces a number of lineside pictures taken on the 5¼ mile section between Enniskillen and Florencecourt. In this picture 'Small Tank' *Hazlewood* is hauling the usual bogie coach No 9 and a brake van. There were no wagons this particular evening.
J L Stevenson

Bottom: *Sir Henry* hauling the 6 30am goods from Sligo on 5th July 1957 has just passed No 1 crossing, Lisgoole, on the approach to Enniskillen. Bogie brake coach No 9 is coupled inside the brake van to form the passenger accommodation on the 7.20pm mixed that evening. This also indicated that a second goods trains from Sligo will be running later that day. When the second goods train did not run the 7.20pm ex-Enniskillen was operated by a railbus sent empty from Sligo.
J J Smith

Left: **This interesting pair of Saxby and Farmer signals, two fishtail arms at the same level pivoted inside a slotted post, was situated between Nos 1 and 2 level crossings. Signals were provided at level crossings between stations to indicate whether the gates were open or shut, except where drivers were considered to have a good view of the gates from some distance away. The signal arms were not interlocked with the gates. This picture also gives us a close look at SLNCR track. Rail lengths were up to 45ft, the original weight of the rails ranged from 75 to 85lbs per yard.** Author

Centre: **In much the same area is railbus 2A, with trailer, working the 1.45pm Enniskillen to Sligo service on 25th May 1955. Out in the countryside the similarity between a railbus and a road bus going along a country lane is more marked. Inside the vehicle the basic differences from a road bus were the sound and feel of rail joints and a driver without a steering wheel!** Author

Bottom: **No 3 crossing was at Mullaghy, four miles from Enniskillen. This was the location of an intermediate halt that was reported in June 1918 as having been, 'cleared away'. The opening date is not recorded but may have been in 1886-87 when other such halts, or market platforms as they were sometimes known, were opened. Heading west in the sunshine of a long summer evening is the 7.20pm mixed from Enniskillen on 25th June 1957, with 0-6-4T 'Large Tank' *Enniskillen* in charge and bogie coach No 10 or 11 immediately behind the locomotive.** Author

Opposite page:

Top: **The 1¼-mile section from Mullaghy to Florencecourt included a climb with sections of 1 in 50 and 1 in 66. *Sir Henry* is commencing this climb in June 1956 with the afternoon goods from Enniskillen to Sligo.** Author

Bottom: **On 25th May 1955, 0-6-4T *Lough Erne* has the 2.15pm Enniskillen to Sligo goods train. The location is two miles out of Enniskillen.** Author

FLORENCECOURT STATION

Top: **Florencecourt station building and its typical Saxby and Farmer SLNCR signal box are shown in this picture of an up goods train exchanging staffs or tickets. The locomotive is thought to be** *Lough Erne* **and the date towards the end of the line's operation. This station, 5¼ miles from Enniskillen, was located merely at the** point where the line crossed a public road, (No 4 gates) there being no village of this name although a Florencecourt post office is recorded. Florence Court is the name of a Georgian mansion some three miles to the south, home of the Earl of Enniskillen, one of the promoters of the line. SLNCR signal boxes, such as that here at Florencecourt, housed only the lever frames. The staff boxes and the telegraph and block instruments for working the line were located in the Station Masters' offices.
Walter Brady collection

Above: **Florencecourt, seen from the rear of an Enniskillen bound train on 15th August 1957. The layout was simple with, on the left, a single siding alongside a goods shed, reached by a crossover at the Enniskillen end. One of the traffics handled here in later years was tar and bitumen, sent in drums from Belfast for Fermanagh County Council. The duo-directional signal on the right has arms with a single red spectacle, the unobscured white light of the signal lamp indicating 'all clear' when the arm was lowered.** A E Bennett

Top: **This unusual and animated scene at Florencecourt on 21st July 1954 resulted from railcar B failing beyond the station, in the Sligo direction, while working the 12 noon service from Enniskillen. It had to be rescued by 0-6-4 tank *Lough Erne* sent specially from Enniskillen. The locomotive hauled railcar B back to the station where passengers, as seen here, had to detrain. They were taken forward eventually on the 1.50pm Enniskillen to Sligo railbus.**
Colin Hogg

Above: **This picture shows a Sligo bound train leaving Florencecourt, with the signal box visible to the right. The train is the 12 noon Enniskillen to Sligo on Saturday 6th July 1957, with 'Large Tank' *Enniskillen* hauling three CIE ex-MGWR 6-wheel coaches, two covered vans and a brake van, instead of being worked by the customary railcar B. The substitution of a steam train on this occasion was due to the anticipated number of passengers which was expected to be in excess of the capacity of the railcar.** J J Smith

BELCOO & BLACK LION

Far left: **Between Florencecourt and Belcoo was an intermediate halt at Abohill, 8¼ miles from Enniskillen. This opened in 1886 and comprised a platform and shelter on the down side of the line. Next came this down distant signal for Belcoo, another single-spectacle arm, but without lamp or glass when photographed on 5th June 1956. Although the arm is a fishtail, the sighting bar is vertical.** Author

Left: **In 1908 Belcoo was renamed Belcoo & Black Lion, the latter being a village in County Cavan, half a mile away, across the River Macnean. This led to an unusual situation from 1922 onwards when Belcoo, in County Fermanagh, remained in the United Kingdom, while Cavan with the village of Blacklion became part of the Irish Free State. This station thus served communities in two different states. It will be noted that the station nameboard, photographed on 30th May 1954, splits the name of the County Cavan village into two separate words. The normal spelling, and that used in SLNCR train and bus timetables, was Blacklion.** Author

Centre left: **Belcoo station was 12¼ miles from Enniskillen. This view, looking in the direction of Enniskillen, shows the double track through the station, its up and down platforms, the water tank and Saxby and Farmer signal box. The up starting signal is another single-spectacle arm. On the left is the goods siding, and the nearer of two leads to the siding from the up line. Beyond the siding was the site of a quarry from which the SLNCR obtained much of its ballast during the line's construction. The quarry continued to be used until some time after the First World War. It was at this quarry that the SLNCR 0-4-0 saddle tank *Faugh a Ballagh* started its career as a contractor's locomotive. This photograph dates from June 1956.** Author

Opposite page:

Top: **This view of an up train at Belcoo shows on the right the rail served end of the goods shed. The train is the 4.00pm Sligo to Enniskillen on 21st July 1954, the day when railcar B failed at Florencecourt (see page 29) when working the 12 noon from Enniskillen. The railcar was therefore unable to take up its booked return service, the 4.00pm from Sligo. In its place a scratch set consisting of SLNCR six-wheel coach No 2, a CIE ex-MGWR six-wheeler and SLNCR six-wheel brake Third No 4, was pressed into service hauled by 0-6-4 tank *Lough Melvin*.** Colin Hogg

Above: **The eastern approach to Belcoo, the down home signal and, on the right, the down passing loop, as seen from the cab of *Lough Melvin* on an up goods train on 5th July 1955.** Lance King

Above: **This photograph shows customs officials inspecting the luggage and parcels in the trailer of railbus 2A which has halted at Belcoo while working the 1.45pm service from Enniskillen to Sligo.** L Hyland, Michael Davies collection

Right: **This view of Belcoo station from the Sligo end, taken on 30th May 1954, shows the level crossing, No 6 gates, station buildings, including those provided from 1923 onwards for H M Customs, and, on the left, the goods shed served by the siding on the up side at the Enniskillen end. The station also housed Belcoo post office.** Author

Above: **A well-loaded 2.15pm Enniskillen to Sligo goods train stands at Belcoo behind 0-6-4T *Lough Erne* in May 1954. It will be seen that the single spectacle down starting signal is devoid of a lamp.** Rev R W A Jones

Left: **Also in May 1954 the 10.30am Sligo to Enniskillen goods climbs the 1 in 50 bank into Belcoo station, to pass *Lough Erne* on the down goods seen in the previous picture. The locomotive is either *Sir Henry* or *Enniskillen*. In a dip between this 1 in 50 climb and another section of 1 in 50 lay the bridge over the River Macnean and the Northern Ireland border. The Belcoo up home signal, shown in this picture, was visible from some distance and drivers of up goods trains seeing the signal on would stop a mile away, and not proceed until the signal was cleared. This enabled them to gather momentum down into the dip, over the river bridge and up the gradient into Belcoo, rather than run the risk of being held at the signal itself and being unable to start on the steep gradient.** Rev R W A Jones

FROM BELCOO TO GLENFARNE

Right: **The section from Belcoo to Glenfarne was five miles long. Shortly after leaving Belcoo, the line passed into the Irish Republic. The first four miles were in County Cavan. There was no SLNCR station in Cavan, but several level crossings. This picture shows the gatehouse at No 7 crossing, Killycarney, two miles beyond Belcoo. Most gatehouses were located on the down side of the line though this was one of seven on the up side. This view was taken on 25th April 1959, after the line had closed, there is already some wire mesh across the track.** Desmond Coakham

Below right: **Nos 8, 9 and 10 crossings were close together. Between Nos 9 and 10 was this remarkable signal, being passed by 0-6-4T *Lough Melvin* on the afternoon Enniskillen to Sligo goods on a wet 16th May 1956, with No 9 gatehouse, at Thornhill crossing, in the background. The two signals in the off position for the down train relate, left, to No 9 crossing (which the train has already passed) and, right, to No 10 crossing which the train is approaching. The signal for up trains, in the on position in this picture, relates to No 8 crossing, that is not the crossing immediately ahead, but the one beyond it.** John Dewing

Below: **This final view of the Belcoo to Glenfarne section gives a good impression of the countryside the line traversed. It was in fact taken on the immediate approach to Glenfarne station and shows 'Small Tank' *Lissadell* on a down train on 6th August 1937.** Robert Fysh collection

GLENFARNE

Top: **This photograph taken from the level crossing, No 12 gates, shows from the Enniskillen end of Glenfarne station, the single platform and station buildings with railbus 2A and trailer on the 6.20am Sligo to Enniskillen service on 26th September 1957. On the platform are tables for the examination of luggage by customs officials. Beyond the trailer can be seen the signal box, and on the right, the loop serving the goods shed.** R Hughes

Centre: **Glenfarne station, 17¼ miles from Enniskillen, was just inside County Leitrim. From 1923 it was used by the Irish Customs to examine trains. This photograph, taken on 18th May 1950, with railcar B just visible on the left, is from the station platform, looking towards Enniskillen across the level crossing. There are two distinctive signals to be seen, the up signal on the left has no spectacle or lamp, while the down signal has the lamp at a lower level than the arm. Both signals are on lattice posts. The approach to Glenfarne from this direction involved a half mile climb into the station, including sections at 1 in 50.** H C Casserley

Left: **The 7.20pm mixed from Enniskillen to Sligo stands at Glenfarne on 15th June 1957, formed of 0-6-4T *Sir Henry*, bogie brake coach No 9 and a brake van. The goods shed is to the left of the locomotive.** Michael Davies

Top: **Glenfarne was not laid out as a passing point, the signalling was arranged only for trains in either direction to use the single platform line. The loop alongside the goods shed did allow passing to take place, although special regulations applied. On 8th June 1957, *Enniskillen* is on the 11.15am to Enniskillen in the loop in the left of the picture, whilst *Lough Melvin* is standing on the main running line with the 2.00pm goods from Enniskillen.** Lance King

Above: ***Lough Erne* shunts the 2.15pm Enniskillen to Sligo goods at Glenfarne on 20th May 1954. In the early 1920s there was a steam-worked 2ft gauge line which conveyed timber from sawmills on the Glenfarne Hall estate, north of the SLNCR line, to Glenfarne station for onward transit mainly to Belfast. This line terminated at the goods platform where *Lough Erne* is standing.**
S C Nash

Top: **0-6-4T *Lough Erne* stands by Glenfarne signal box in May 1954 with the 2.15pm Enniskillen to Sligo goods. To the left of the second wagon in the train can be seen the buffer stop of a siding, diverging from the loop, which served an end-loading dock.**
Rev R W A Jones

Above: **Looking west from Glenfarne on 18th May 1950 we see the line resuming its climb, to Kilmakerrill summit some 4½ miles farther on. Wagons are standing in the end-loading dock and, far right, on the loop serving the goods shed.**
H C Casserley

KILMAKERRILL SUMMIT

Below: **The climb, in either direction, to Kilmakerrill summit, 367ft above sea level, was the feature of the 7½ miles section from Glenfarne to Manorhamilton. Just east of the summit, at No 14 level crossing, was Kilmakerrill Halt, opened on 28th July 1929, 21¼ miles from Enniskillen. In this picture, taken on 26th June 1955, railbus 2A and trailer have just passed No 13 gates at Cornacloy. The railbus was having problems ascending the bank on wet rails**

and the photographer was able to alight from the slow-moving train, walk ahead to take this photograph and then board the train again! Peter Gray

Bottom left: **This picture portrays the aftermath of the most serious malicious incident to affect the SLNCR during the 1923 disturbances. It shows 'Small Tank' *Hazlewood* which had been derailed whilst descending from Kilmakerrill summit to Glenfarne with an up train on 3rd April. The locomotive was reported to have rolled over twice falling down the embankment. It landed upright, 66ft from the line and 36ft below it.** H Taylor collection

Bottom right: **Steam hauled passenger trains, other than the famed 7.20pm mixed from Enniskillen, were rare on the SLNCR in the 1950s, running only as substitutes for the railcar or railbuses, or as special excursions. One such excursion from Enniskillen to Sligo and back was on the last Sunday of each July and was known as the Garland Sunday or the Holy Well excursion. The final such excursion, on 28th July 1957, is shown here at Kilmakerrill Halt, hauled by *Sir Henry*. It will be seen that the halt was located on the up side of the line, on the Sligo side of the level crossing.**
Drew Donaldson, W T Scott collection

This sequence of pictures was taken on 24th May 1955.
The train is the 11.15am Sligo to Enniskillen goods on the
climb to Kilmakerrill, shortly after leaving Manorhamilton,
on a section of the line with gradients as steep as 1 in 50.
The locomotive is 'Small Tank' *Hazlewood*, hauling 15 wagons,
empty bogie coach No 11 and 7 ton brake van No 1. Coach No 11
can be distinguished from the almost identical No.10, which had
no electric lighting, by the wiring conduit along the clerestory.
The coach is being conveyed to provide passenger accommodation
on the 7.20pm mixed from Enniskillen later in the day. Author

MANORHAMILTON

Manorhamilton, 24¾ miles from Enniskillen, was not only the most important intermediate station and the mid-way point between Enniskillen and Sligo, it was also the SLNCR's engineering centre, with locomotive, carriage and wagon shops. From 1891, the company's engineer was based here as well.

Top: **On 22nd June 1955, *Lough Melvin* approaches Manorhamilton with the 2.15pm Enniskillen to Sligo goods. The Saxby and Farmer down home signal protected the level crossing, No 17 gates, at the Enniskillen end of the station and entry into the down platform.** Peter Gray

Right: **Locomotives were invariably turned at Enniskillen and Sligo, thus pictures of bunker first running are rare. This special train of empty cattle wagons approaching Manorhamilton behind *Sir Henry*, on 27th May 1953, was worked in this fashion because the locomotive was then a spare based at Manorhamilton. All locomotives, either for repair or as spares, usually** entered Manorhamilton works facing Enniskillen. This meant that when called upon to take special cattle trains from Collooney to Enniskillen, Manorhamilton based locomotives had the sanding apparatus, which was located ahead of the leading driving wheel, available for the climb out of Collooney. The crew on *Sir Henry* in this picture are Tommy McTernan and Paddy Hugh Keaney. Author

Top: **On the down side adjacent to the level crossing was the carriage and wagon shop. On 18th May 1950 railbus A passes this building on an Enniskillen to Sligo working.** H C Casserley

Above: **The end of the carriage and wagon shop is just visible as *Lough Melvin* enters the down platform line at Manorhamilton with the Enniskillen to Sligo goods on 14th August 1957. The carriage and wagon shop** was at the end of a storage siding running behind the entire length of the down platform. **This shop may have originally accommodated two tracks though latterly there was only one.** Desmond Coakham

Above: **This is a general view of Manorhamilton, photographed from the level crossing, looking westwards, on 29th June 1938. The down platform is on the left, with the signal box at its far end. The goods shed is in the centre of the picture and the principal station buildings are on the up platform on the right of the photographer.** H C Casserley

Centre: **A picture few photographers would have bothered to take, a view of the station approach and forecourt at Manorhamilton on 29th June 1938. The main station building is in the centre, with, on its left side, the awning over the up platform. On the very far left can be seen one end of the roof of the carriage shed behind the down platform.** H C Casserley

Right: *Lissadell* **takes water at Manorhamilton on 29th June 1938 while hauling the 10.20am train from Sligo to Enniskillen. Passenger accommodation is provided by bogie clerestory coach No 9. As this train had a 2hrs 10min schedule it is highly unlikely to have run as a mixed train, the wagons at the rear are therefore probably vacuum braked vehicles suitable for use on passenger trains. Just visible in this picture are the window lights in the clerestory of coach No 9. Similar lights were in the clerestories of the other bogie coaches, Nos 10 and 11. All were later covered over, as may be noted from other photos of these carriages elsewhere in the book.** H C Casserley

Above: **This photograph, taken from the up platform on 14th August 1957, shows the nameboard on the down platform, the Engineer's offices on the embankment behind the station and the signal box. Visible on the storage siding behind the down platform are, from left to right, six-wheel Third class saloon brake coach No 4, cattle wagon No 59, brake van No 3, which had a compartment for drovers, and bogie coach No 10. Beyond the signal box is cattle wagon No 154.** Desmond Coakham

Centre: **Another view of Manorhamilton's down platform and the storage siding behind it, taken in June 1953. At the far left can be seen the end of the carriage and wagon shop, to the left of the waiting shelter. This picture also shows clearly the carriage shed structure over the storage siding and the Engineer's residence is in view on the embankment. The two coaches outside the carriage shed are, left, No 4 and six-wheel Third class brake No 15, which had a Ladies Only compartment on its own beyond the brake compartment. No 15, which at one time had a birdcage lookout above the brake compartment, was sold for scrap in 1954.** Rev R W A Jones

Left: **GNR A class 0-6-0 No 28 stands by the signal box on a down freight. This engine was on loan to the SLNCR from October 1950 to July 1951 while the company was awaiting the arrival of the two new Beyer Peacock 0-6-4 tanks, *Lough Melvin* and *Lough Erne*.** David Murray collection

Top: **Leaving Manorhamilton on 29th June 1938 was GNR railbus E working the 10.15am Enniskillen to Sligo service. The temporary use of a GNR vehicle, which incidentally does not have a luggage trailer, may be related to the introduction of a two railbus timetable from 1st June of that year which was followed eight days later by damage to the company's most recently acquired railbus, 2A. Above the railbus again can be seen the residence of the SLNCR engineer, by this time G F Egan, who held the post from 1925 until the line closed.** H C Casserley

Above left: A wide-ranging group of SLNCR staff pose for the camera on the down platform at Manorhamilton in a photograph thought to date from 1951. From left to right are Paddy Nevin, the Enniskillen-based driver who usually drove railcar B, John Ward, Station Foreman at Manorhamilton, Harry Taylor Chief Clerk at Enniskillen who later, from 1st June 1956 assumed the role of Traffic Manager, Jack McGee Station Master at Manorhamilton, Mick Walsh, Road Supervisor, Ernie Monahan, Accountant and

later from 1st March 1956 General Manager and Secretary as well, and Gerard F Egan, the SLNCR's Engineer for over 30 years and a good friend to people interested in the railway.
Pauric McKeon collection

Above right: **Signalman Seamus McTernan stands by the lever frame in Manorhamilton signal box on 4th July 1955. A Saxby and Farmer builders plate can be observed behind the frame, to the right of the picture.** Lance King

Above: **Looking west at Manorhamilton, railcar B arrives with the 4.00pm Sligo to Enniskillen service on 24th May 1955. On the left is coach No 10 and in front of it we see Manorhamilton's distinctive down starting signal.** Author

Bottom: **Turning around almost immediately, on 24th May 1955, railcar B at the up platform at Manorhamilton, with a fair number of passengers joining and alighting. The white tailboard at the back of the railcar, was used by some Irish railways instead of a tail lamp, to mark the last vehicle of a train in daylight.** Author

Opposite page, top.
Hazlewood is shunting the 9.00am from Sligo at the goods shed on the up side of the running lines on 27th May 1953. The track through the shed commenced at a loading dock behind the photographer and was reached by two crossovers from the up running line. One of these was the crossover on which *Hazlewood* is standing, the other was beyond the goods shed. The track then continued westwards, past the locomotive shops terminating in a corrugated iron storage shed. Two leads from this track entered the locomotive shops at the Sligo end. Author

Above: **At the other end of Manorhamilton goods shed, *Lough Erne* is shunting the 2.00pm Enniskillen to Sligo goods train on 7th September 1957. On the right the two platform lines are merging** into the single track towards Dromahair, behind them is the carriage and wagon storage line. Peter Hay

Above: **It had to be mid-summer to photograph the 7.20pm mixed from Enniskillen as far west as Manorhamilton, where it was due at 8 30pm. This picture, with *Sir Henry* at the head and numerous cattle wagons behind, dates from 6th June 1956. Wagon No 151 on the right of the locomotive is unusual, being a ventilated van, converted from a cattle wagon.** Author

Below: **This photo shows the Garland Sunday excursion of 29th July 1956 at Manorhamilton on its outwards run from Enniskillen to Sligo. *Lough Erne* is hauling a bogie non-corridor clerestory coach hired from the GNR and the SLNCR's three bogie clerestory coaches, with No 9, the brake composite, at the rear.** Author

Above: **Before it was bought by the SLNCR, the 0-6-0 No 79 was renumbered 69 by the GNR. This picture shows the engine at Manorhamilton with its new identity. It is outside the corrugated iron shed referred to in an earlier caption, at the end of the track serving the locomotive shops. This photograph presumably dates from 1940 after the locomotive's purchase by the SLNCR but before it was named *Sligo*, the line's second 0-6-0 to carry this name.**
Charles Friel collection

Right: **By way of contrast, this is an earlier photograph of the same locomotive when it was numbered 79 and was on loan to the SLNCR. Taken at Manorhamilton on 29th July 1936, it is standing on the main line, to the west of the locomotive shops.**
R G Jarvis, courtesy Midland Railway Centre Museum collection

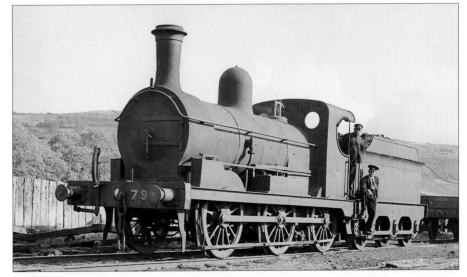

Bottom: **A view looking east, taken on 27th May 1953, of Manorhamilton's locomotive shops and station approach from the Sligo end. On the right is the main running line, with the up home signal and station visible in the centre. On the left is the track which has come through the goods shed, the gable end of which can be seen above the roof of cattle wagon No 157. On the far left are the two tracks leading into the locomotive shops. Outside the shops are *Lissadell* on the left and the luggage trailer from railbus A on the right.** Author

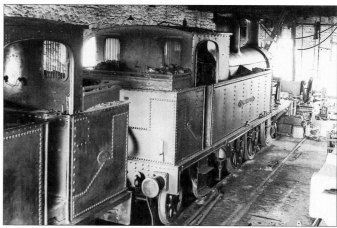

Above left: **This is a closer view of the exterior of the locomotive shops, with three 0-6-4Ts in view, a 'Large Tank' on the left, and two 'Small Tanks' on the right hand road, all facing Enniskillen.** John Langford collection

Above right: **'Large Tank' *Enniskillen* is on the outermost of the two roads in Manorhamilton shops in this interior view. Beyond the locomotive is some of the equipment which even the Engineer admitted was old and rather out-of-date.**

The late R N Clements, a respected authority on Irish steam locomotives, described Manorhamilton shops as 'one of the last homes of craftsmanship'. Next to *Enniskillen* can be seen the cab and bunker of another of the three 'Large Tanks', in this case unusually, for Manorhamilton shops, facing Sligo rather than Enniskillen. Lens of Sutton

Below: *Hazlewood* inside the works on the road nearer the main running line, on 14th August 1957. Desmond Coakham

MANORHAMILTON TO DROMAHAIR

The 8½ mile section between Manorhamilton and Dromahair stations was punctuated by a halt at Lisgorman, 4¾ miles from Manorhamilton at milepost 29½. Lisgorman was opened in 1887 but it was decided to close it in 1917 and to clear the platform away. However, a halt was later re-introduced in 1940, but without a platform, passengers joining the railbuses and later the railcar, by steps from ground level. For this reason steam trains did not call there.

Top: **Railcar B is on the 9.30am, summer timetable only, Sligo to Enniskillen service on the approach to Manorhamilton in this view from 27th May 1953. Although the Manorhamilton to Dromahair section was mostly undulating, there was a steady 1 in 53 climb towards Manorhamilton from the Sligo direction.** Author

Centre: **In more open country, 'Small Tank' *Lurganboy* is nearing Manorhamilton with the 9.45am Sligo to Enniskillen goods on 30th June 1950.** John Edgington

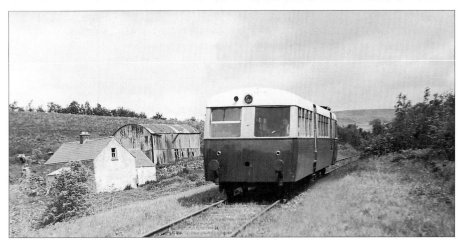

Right: **In this photo, railcar B is west of Manorhamilton on the 12 noon Enniskillen to Sligo service on 27th May 1953.** Author

Top: **Cleen level crossing, No 18 gates, was within a mile of Dromahair station. The crossing's gatehouse and the adjacent bridge over the River Bonet are in the left background of this view of railcar B on the 12 noon Enniskillen to Sligo service on 29th June 1957. The signal in the foreground is the up signal for Cleen crossing and is another unusual one, its arm attached to a telegraph pole!** Author

Above: **There were numerous curves, with speed restrictions to match, on the approach to Dromahair from the Manor-hamilton direction as the line followed the River Bonet. In this view, one of the 'Lough' 0-6-4Ts on an Enniskillen to Sligo goods train is alongside the river on a section known as Parson's Curve east of Cleen level crossing.**
L. Hyland, Michael Davies collection

Right: **Another notable signal was at the top of a cutting on the approach to Dromahair station from the Manor-hamilton direction. The unusual nature of this signal derived from the practice of trains passing at Dromahair although there was no loop there, the layout merely comprising, in addition to the main running line, a two road goods yard and shunting neck, reached by a crossover which was facing for down trains. The upper conventional arm, relatively** speaking for it had a slotted post and only one spectacle and its lamp was at a lower level than the arm, was the down outer home, although the arm bore trace of at one time having been a fishtail distant. The lower arm was the up advanced starting signal which, signified by the cross on the sighting bar on the reverse of the signal arm, also functioned as a shunt back signal for long up goods trains reversing into the yard for shunting or to cross another train. J J Smith

DROMAHAIR STATION

Top: **Dromahair was 33¼ miles from Enniskillen. This picture, taken from the Enniskillen end, shows the 9.00am Sligo to Enniskillen goods being worked by** *Hazlewood*, **shunting there on 24th June 1953. The main part of the train, headed by cattle wagon No 36, is at the station platform, while the locomotive is on the outer track of the two road goods yard alongside the two goods sheds. The signal box, although of traditional Saxby and Farmer outline, was in fact rebuilt after being maliciously damaged by fire in 1923.** J J Smith

Centre: **The goods yard is seen here from the opposite direction in this picture taken over the wall at the back of the station platform, looking towards Enniskillen, on 27th September 1957.** Desmond Coakham

Right: **A level crossing, No 19 gates, was at the Sligo end of Dromahair station. This view, taken on 18th May 1950, is from the level crossing, looking towards Enniskillen. On the left is the platform with the two storey station, unique for the SLNCR whose other station buildings were single storey affairs. The signal box is at the far end of the platform.** H C Casserley

Left: **The train which the people seen in the previous view were awaiting is seen in this photograph of railbus 2A and trailer on a Sligo to Enniskillen service at Dromahair on 18th May 1950. Both pictures suggest that a knot of people are seeing a passenger off, perhaps someone emigrating, an event not uncommon in these parts in the 1950s.** H C Casserley

Centre: **This picture of railcar B at Dromahair gives a closer view of the cowling which it sometimes sported around the cooling apparatus above the driving cab.** Charles Friel collection

Bottom: *Lough Melvin* **pauses at Dromahair on 23rd June 1953 with an Enniskillen to Sligo goods. This view also shows the level crossing gates and the down starting signal which, true to the unusual standards of SLNCR signalling which will have been noted as we have progressed down the line, had only one spectacle and no lamp.** J J Smith

WEST OF DROMAHAIR

Above: **Immediately west of Dromahair station the line ran in an attractive setting along an avenue of trees, through which *Lough Erne* brings the 2.00pm Enniskillen to Sligo goods train on 7th September 1957.** Peter Hay

Right: **This interesting set of signals, with the lamp at a higher level than the arms, protected one of the eight intermediate level crossings on the 8¼ mile section from Dromahair to Collooney. There were two intermediate calling points between these stations. Ballintogher, the first in County Sligo, was 36¼ miles from Enniskillen. It was rather more than a halt as it had a goods store. Ballygawley Halt, 39¾ miles from Enniskillen, was the other stopping place on this part of the line. This photograph dates from 19th May 1959, after the closure of the railway.** Desmond Coakham

BALLINTOGHER

Above: **The 9.45am Sligo to Enniskillen goods, hauled by 0-6-4T *Lough Gill* stands at Ballintogher on 1st July 1953. In the foreground is the level crossing, No 24 gates, and on the left is the crossing keeper's house, the occupant of which issued tickets. On the platform is the two-way level crossing signal, in the off position. It will be seen that when viewed by down trains, the signal points the wrong way, to the right rather than to the left, a characteristic of a number of SLNCR signals. This section of line opened in 1881 and Ballintogher was appearing in timetables by January 1883. The goods store, which distinguished Ballintogher from the other intermediate halts or market platforms as they were sometimes called on the SLNCR, was added in 1902. Though goods trains called, there was no siding here. In later years Ballintogher was classified as a halt, with passenger trains calling only on request. *Lough Gill* was the third and final 'Large Tank'. Built by Beyer Peacock (works No 5943), it entered service in 1917. Although in traffic stock until the line's closure, the loco was actually at Dundalk works awaiting repairs when services on the SLNCR ended.**
J J Smith

Above: **Another high mid-summer picture of the 7.20pm from Enniskillen, this time as far west as Ballintogher on 10th July 1957, taken at around 9.00pm. The photograph again shows the two-way signal which had a white sighting bar on either side of the signal arm. This view also gives us a sight of Ballintogher's not very impressive goods store. The locomotive is *Lough Erne* and the passenger coach is No 9.** Drew Donaldson, W T Scott collection

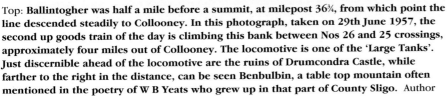

Below: **This signal, pointing the wrong way for down trains, protected No 27 level crossing, Castle Dargan, three miles beyond Ballintogher. The gate house is in the distance.** Desmond Coakham

Top: **Ballintogher was half a mile before a summit, at milepost 36¾, from which point the line descended steadily to Collooney. In this photograph, taken on 29th June 1957, the second up goods train of the day is climbing this bank between Nos 26 and 25 crossings, approximately four miles out of Collooney. The locomotive is one of the 'Large Tanks'. Just discernible ahead of the locomotive are the ruins of Drumcondra Castle, while farther to the right in the distance, can be seen Benbulbin, a table top mountain often mentioned in the poetry of W B Yeats who grew up in that part of County Sligo.** Author

Above: **Ballygawley Halt, 39¾ miles from Enniskillen, photographed from the rear of an up goods train on 5th July 1955. The decision to build Ballygawley Halt was reached in December 1886, but it appears that the halt may have been closed for a while during the years preceding the First World War. As at the other halts, there was no lighting here.** Lance King

COLLOONEY

Top: Collooney station, 41½ miles from Enniskillen was the final one on the SLNCR. Seen here, from the east end on 25th August 1956, on the right are the two platforms, up starting signal, water tower and signal box. On the left is the three-road goods yard. The goods shed, visible to the right of brake van No 2, was between the outermost and centre lines, while the innermost line faced a cattle dock behind the down platform. The outermost line, left, also fronted a long cattle loading platform, and this line continued behind the camera to a headshunt which, until about 1925, terminated in a small shed for a banking and shunting locomotive, usually 0-6-0T *Waterford*. The yard was reached by two crossovers. One facing Enniskillen is in the centre of this picture, at the end of the down platform. The second crossover, facing Sligo, led off the down platform line and can be seen running into the bottom of the photograph, right of centre. Desmond Coakham

Above: *Lough Gill* stands on the innermost road of Collooney goods yard in June 1953 while working the 9.00am Sligo to Enniskillen goods. The cattle dock platform can be seen to the right, with the wall separating the dock from the down platform. To the left of the train is the goods shed. Rev R W A Jones

Right: **Collooney was the major source of the SLNCR's most important traffic, that of cattle. This frequently necessitated special trains to Enniskillen. In this atmospheric picture, the second 0-6-0 *Sligo* is getting away from Collooney with a scheduled Sligo to Enniskillen goods train in May 1947.** John Dewing

Centre: **Collooney from the Sligo end on 25th August 1956, showing the up and down platforms and lines and revealing that, unlike other SLNCR stations, whose buildings were made of stone, those at Collooney were of timber and corrugated iron construction. In accordance with standard SLNCR practice, the staff box, telegraph and block instruments for the section to Dromahair were housed in the Station Master's office. However, from 1930, when the GSR took out Carrignagat Junction at the end of the SLNCR line and instituted parallel single line working thence to Ballysodare, the new Collooney to Ballysodare section was worked by a GSR electric train staff system. The instruments and telephone used to work the section were installed in the SLNCR signal box at Collooney.** Desmond Coakham

Below: **Railbus A pauses at Collooney whilst working an Enniskillen to Sligo service on 14th August 1957.** Desmond Coakham

Above: **This picture of railcar B entering Collooney from Sligo on 25th August 1956 features the level crossing, No 28 gates, the final one on the SLNCR, with beyond it the girder bridge over the Owenmore River.** Desmond Coakham

Left: **At the farther end of the Owenmore River bridge, the girders of which flank this picture, was the junction with the 46 chain spur, owned by the W&LR and its successors, leading to the ex-W&LR Collooney station and the line thence to Claremorris. The W&LR and its successors contributed to the installation of the junction and also to the costs of working and maintaining it. The spur, known as the 'Southern siding', was little used after the formation of the GSR and from 1944 was used only for wagon storage, as seen in this picture taken on 25th August 1956, with SLNCR cattle wagon No 130 nearest the camera. The SLNCR line continues, right, towards Carrignagat Junction, Ballysodare and Sligo.** Desmond Coakham

SHARED TRACKS

Top left: **Carrignagat Junction, 42 miles and 50 chains from Enniskillen, and the point at which the SLNCR joined the MGWR, is seen here after the SLNCR line had been lifted, leaving only the ex-MGWR line in situ. On the right is the MGWR 128¾ milepost, measured from their Dublin Broadstone terminus. This was the official measurement for Carrignagat Junction. The SLNCR had paid for the cost of installing the junction, including the signal box and the double cottage, in the centre of the picture, for two signalmen. The SLNCR also bore the cost of the second track,** which became MGWR property, between the junction and Ballysodare, a distance of approximately one mile. This second track became the up line (until 1930 when the junction was taken out), down trains using the original MGWR single-line.
Michael Davies

Top right: **This picture was taken from the rear of a down SLNCR train between Carrignagat Junction and Ballysodare in 1953. The left-hand track is that used by the SLNCR, CIE trains used the other road. The signals on the right are for CIE trains approaching Collooney Junction, 57 chains south of the site of Carrignagat Junction, where the lines to Dublin and Claremorris diverged.** H C Casserley

Above: **A Sligo bound SLNCR train enters Ballysodare, hauled by one of the 'Small Tanks', thought to be *Fermanagh*, which along with *Leitrim*, were the first Beyer Peacock 0-6-4Ts, dating from 1882. *Fermanagh* lasted until 1952 when it was withdrawn and sold for scrap. Coaches 3 and 4 lead the train's mixed formation. This picture is from the post-1930 period. The train is therefore coming off the single track used by SLNCR trains from Carrignagat Junction which has run alongside the other line used by GSR trains. The train is negotiating the crossover leading to what is the down line through Ballysodare station. From here there was a conventional double track section to Sligo.** John Langford collection

Above: **On 27th September 1957 railbus 2A and trailer are at the down platform at Ballysodare on the 1.45pm Enniskillen to Sligo service. Behind the railbus is the GSR signal box, in front of which stand the up splitting signals, the left-hand arm being that for SLNCR trains, the right hand arm controlling CIE trains onto the parallel single line on which some wagons are** standing, **towards the site of Carrignagat Junction and then to Collooney Junction where the former MGWR and WL&WR routes diverged.** Desmond Coakham

Below: **On the double track section approaching Ballysodare from the Sligo direction, is the return Holy Well excursion** from Sligo to Enniskillen on 29th July 1956. This train on its outward journey, was recorded at Manorhamilton in an earlier photograph, see page 46. *Lough Erne* **is again hauling the train. The formation has been remarshalled so that, as on the outward journey, the GNR coach is immediately behind the locomotive and SLNCR bogie brake No 9 is at rear.** Author

SLIGO

Above: *Enniskillen* poses in front of Sligo station's GSR bilingual station nameboard, during the period when the SLNCR's initials were painted on the sides of locomotives' tanks.
H Fayle, author's collection

Below: **Railcar B is inside Sligo station at the down arrival platform on 5th November 1955.** Desmond Coakham

Left: 'Large Tank' *Sir Henry* stands outside Sligo passenger station on 2nd June 1940 waiting to work a return excursion to Belfast, which was formed of four GNR corridor coaches. The SLNCR tank took the train as far as Enniskillen. Bob O'Sullivan

Centre: This photograph shows details of Sligo passenger station, 48 miles from Enniskillen. The terminal station comprises arrival and departure platform lines with two storage roads between them. It was normal practice for some SLNCR rolling stock to be stabled on one of these carriage sidings. The station was burned down during the 'Troubles' of the early 1920s but was rebuilt in similar style though without the former overall roof. The second railbus A is seen making a smoky departure for Enniskillen. Charles Friel collection

Left: **Railcar B at the departure platform on 3rd September 1957.** Norman Simmons, Photos from the Fifties

Right: **The former MGWR shed at Sligo was used by SLNCR motive power. Photographed here on 6th August 1937 is the original railbus A and trailer.** Robert Fysh collection

Bottom: **This view gives an idea of the structure and size of Sligo locomotive shed as well as showing** Lough Melvin **alongside the water tower on 9th July 1955. On the rear of the bunker can be seen the rectangular plate which stated that Beyer Peacock & Co Ltd were the owners of the locomotive, not the SLNCR.** Lawrence Marshall

Below: **A close-up of the Beyer Peacock owner's plate on the rear of** Lough Melvin's **bunker.** H C Casserley

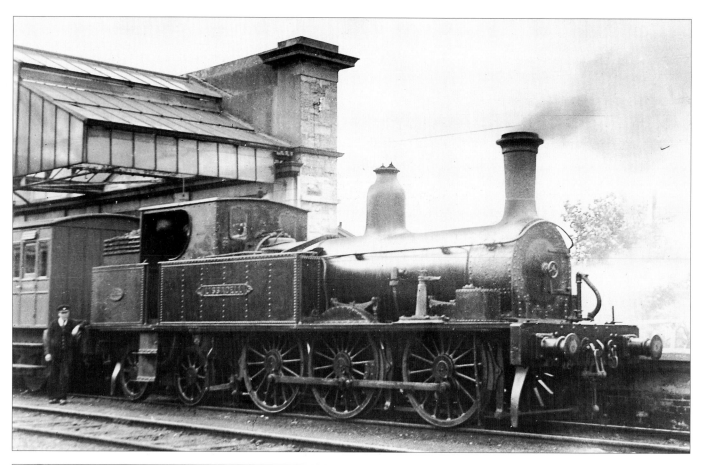

Top: 'Small Tank' *Lissadell*, at the head of a train at Sligo station's departure platform on 20th June 1939. John Dewing

Bottom: **Immediately outside Sligo passenger station is this typical MGWR signal box where the single track to Sligo goods station and Sligo Quay diverged on the down side, the junction facing Ballysodare. This picture shows *Hazlewood* with an Enniskillen bound goods train coming off the Sligo Quay line on 15th May 1956. The tracks to the passenger station are in the foreground.** John Dewing

Top: **The line to Sligo goods station is almost half a mile in length. It falls away from the main line on a gradient of 1 in 70. A further half mile extension to Sligo Quay was the property of the Sligo Harbour Commissioners. In this view *Lough Erne* has arrived at the goods station with the 2.00pm goods from Enniskillen on 7th September 1957. In the right background is the outer wall of Sligo passenger station.** Peter Hay

Above: **Preparing the 11.15am goods to Enniskillen on 5th July 1955 is 0-6-4T *Lough Melvin*. On the adjacent road is SLNCR brake van No.6 and on the right is ex-MGWR E class, now CIE J26 class, 0-6-0T No 558. Sligo was an important source of traffic for the SLNCR. In 1896 its General Manager claimed that his line had largely helped to make Sligo the most, if not the only, thriving seaport on the west coast of Ireland.** Lance King

ROLLING STOCK

Left: Six-wheel coach No 3 was similar to coach No 2, shown in an earlier photograph at Enniskillen (see page 20), in that it had four compartments and had been purchased from the GNR. No 3 differed from No 2 however, in having a double-door luggage compartment between the two inner First class compartments. Its outer compartments were Third class. The vehicle was 30ft in overall length and was purchased from the GNR in 1936, having been GNR No 95. No 3 remained in stock until the line's closure. It is shown here at Enniskillen on 30th May 1954. Author

Centre left: Six-wheel coach No 4, also pictured at Enniskillen on 30th May 1954, had originally been a brake Third with three compartments and a birdcage lookout over the brake compartment. It was altered in the early 1920's into the brake Third saloon shown here. Overall length was 28ft 3in and the vehicle, which had steam heating and electric lighting, was in stock until closure. Author

Bottom: Six-wheel coach No 6, recorded at Enniskillen on 24th June 1937, was 30ft 10½in in overall length. Its six Third class compartments had full-height partitions only between each pair of compartments. The vehicle had no steam heating or electric lighting, but was originally lit by acetylene gas. Coaches Nos 6, 8 and 14 were derelict at Manorhamilton by 1950 and were sold for scrap in 1954. H C Casserley

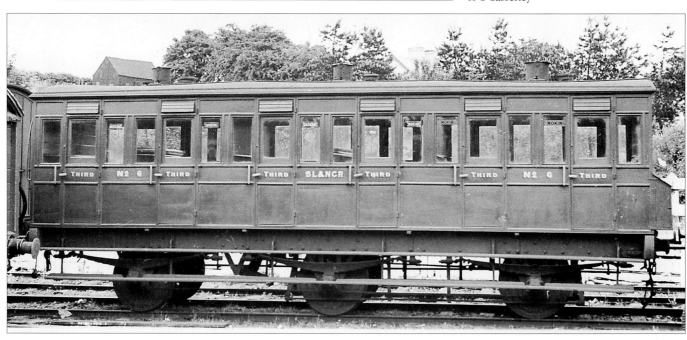

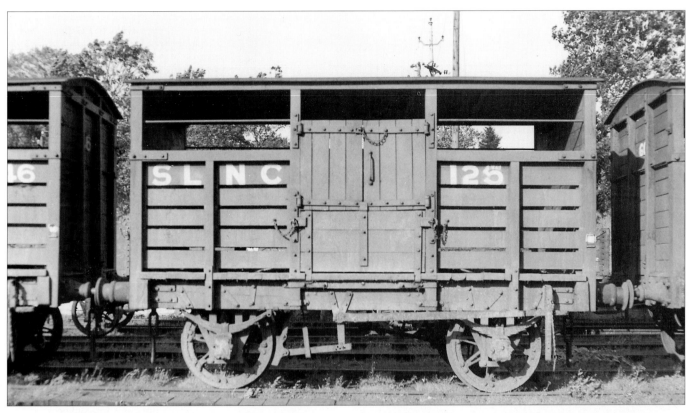

Above: **As might be expected, the largest category in the wagon fleet consisted of cattle wagons, 70 remaining in stock until closure, the majority being of 7-ton capacity. At least 14 cattle wagons were fitted for running in passenger trains. Cattle wagon No 125, photographed at Enniskillen on 24th September 1952, is painted in the standard SLNCR grey wagon livery with white lettering and numerals. Numbers were painted on the ends of vehicles as well as on the sides.** Desmond Coakham

Below: **Brake vans were listed in a separate number sequence. Nos 1, 2, 3, 5 and 6 were still on the books at the closure. This picture, taken at Manorhamilton on 27th May 1953, shows 7-ton van No 2 which had a drovers' compartment at one end and space for some goods in the centre. Brake van No 3 was similar to No 2, although it was recorded as a 10-ton vehicle. Photographs show it with glazed droplights as opposed to No 2's wooden ones.** Author

Left: **There were two carriage trucks recorded in SLNCR stock, also numbered in a separate series, 1 and 2. This photograph, taken at Manorhamilton 19 months after closure, on 18th May 1959, shows one of these trucks up for sale as Lot 53. Originally there was horizontal planking behind the wooden frames along each side of the vehicle. The number was carried on this planking and it is not known therefore, whether this picture shows No 1 or No 2. Latterly the two carriage trucks had been in store in the corrugated iron shed at the western end of the track passing through the goods shed and alongside the locomotive shops at Manorhamilton.** Desmond Coakham

Centre: **Brake van No 5, pictured here at Manorhamilton on 31st May 1954, was a 10-tonner. There was plenty of room for goods in the van.** Author

Bottom: **Brake van No 6, a 7-ton vehicle seen here at Enniskillen on 25th August 1956, was more conventional, with an open verandah at each end and plenty of room for the guard which he did not have to share with merchandise. No 1 was of similar design to No 6.** Desmond Coakham

Top: **Parcels van No 7 was one of four in stock at the closure of the line. The original print is in sepia and is believed to show the vehicle when it was new. These vans had their own number series, screw couplings and were piped or fitted to run in passenger trains.**
H Taylor collection

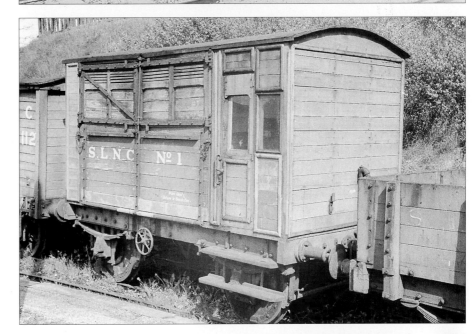

Centre: **The horse box numbered 1 came from the WL&WR as the replacement for the original SLNCR vehicle which was damaged at Sligo. This view was taken at Manorhamilton on 24th May 1955.**
Author

Bottom: **There were 43, 7-ton covered wagons in stock at the closure. No 131 did not appear on the post closure auctioneer's lists, so we can therefore assume that it was one of those sold for scrap in 1954, the year it was recorded at Manorhamilton.**
Author

Top left: **No 145 was one of 28, 7-ton open wagons on the company's books at the time of closure. It was photographed at Manorhamilton on 23rd April 1959, shortly before auction to dispose of the stock gathered there. In this view the wagon is loaded with a container.** Desmond Coakham

Centre left: **In the early 1920s there were 209 goods wagons in the SLNCR stock, although this figure was reduced to 153 by the time of the closure of the line in 1957. As recently as 1954, 50 wagons had been sold for scrap. This photograph shows four-wheel 4½-ton open wagon No 1, the only one of this capacity in stock, when pictured on 16th August 1957 at Enniskillen.** Desmond Coakham

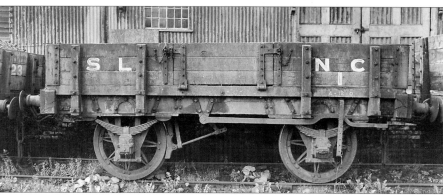

Bottom: **Numbered amongst the goods wagons were two 6-wheel 12-ton low-sided ballast wagons, Nos 5 and 25. No 5, bearing the initials P.W.D (Permanent Way Department) is shown here at Manorhamilton on 25th August 1956. Latterly it was the practice to convey ballast on goods trains and to unload it *en route*, at walking pace, as the train moved slowly along.** Desmond Coakham

BUSES

Top: **Photographs are presented here of six of the nine buses operated by the SLNCR during the period from 1945 to 1957. The fleet at any particular time usually comprised four vehicles. Seen at Manorhamilton on 21st April 1948 is IL2058, a 20-seat Bedford petrol engined bus, dating from 1932, one of the two taken over from Mr Appleby and used on his Blacklion - Manorhamilton - Sligo service at the start of SLNCR bus operations in 1945. This vehicle was scrapped in 1949. SLNCR bus livery was light green and cream. The full extent of the company's bus operations is shown on the bus timetable and route map on page 80.** H C Casserley

Centre: **The other bus which came from Appleby in 1945 was a 26-seat petrol engined Bedford, registration number EI 3905, dating from 1938. This photograph was taken in Sligo in 1948, shortly before it was withdrawn.** Bryan Boyle

Below: **In 1948 two new Commer diesel-engined 32-seater buses were bought to replace the original vehicles taken over from Appleby. One of the new Commers was EI 4907, seen here at Manorhamilton on 15th August 1957.** A E Bennett

Top left: **For the start of its bus operations the company also acquired two petrol-engined buses from the GNR. AZ 1514 of 1928 was a 31-seater, rebodied in 1937 and purchased by the SLNCR in 1946. It is seen here at Sligo. The other bus was ZI 4279, a 32-seater dating from 1929, rebodied in 1938 and bought by the SLNCR in 1945. The GNR fleet numbers had been 296 (later 129) and 96 respectively. After being fitted with diesel engines in 1948, these two buses remained in the SLNCR fleet until 1953.** Bryan Boyle

Top right: **The second Commer purchased in 1948 was EI 5040, pictured here at the bus garage in Manorhamilton on 8th June 1953. Again with the help of Michael Hamilton, the members of staff are identified as John Roche, left, a lorry and bus driver with the SLNCR and, right, Sean Loughlin, a mechanic.** John Gillham

Centre left: **A further view of EI 5040 seen here at Manorhamilton on 4th September 1957. Both Commers remained in the fleet until the cessation of operations at the end of that month.** Keith Walton

Left: **In 1953 two more GNR buses were bought, to replace the ex-GNR vehicles acquired in 1945-46. The 1953 buses were Gardner engined 35-seaters dating from 1937, ZC 1850 (GNR No 214) and ZC 2269 (GNR No 218). ZC 1850 lasted only until 1956 when it was replaced by a similar ex-GNR vehicle ZC 1576 (GNR No 208), shown here at Sligo, which, with ZC 2269, remained in the company's fleet until the end. Regrettably I have not been able to find any illustrations of the SLNCR's lorry fleet. Three lorries or vans were offered for sale when the services closed down in 1957, although in the post war years the fleet had sometimes numbered as many as six vehicles.** Robert Grieves

SLNCR SURVIVORS

Top: **The last two 0-6-4Ts, *Lough Erne* and *Lough Melvin* were sold by Beyer Peacock to the UTA in 1959. Numbered 27 and 26 respectively by the Authority, the latter is seen here on an Irish Railway Record Society special train to Antrim on 11th June 1960. The train which consists of two ex-GNR corridor coaches is between Bleach Green Junction and Monkstown on the former NCC main line from Belfast to Londonderry.** Bob O'Sullivan

Right: **The two ex-SLNCR locomotives were used primarily by the UTA for shunting at goods yards in the Belfast area. This picture shows the now numbered 27, *Lough Erne*, on a goods train near the terminal which served the British Railways shipping service to Heysham, at Donegall Quay in Belfast, on 17th August 1962.** Bob O'Sullivan

Bottom right: **The SLNCR's railcar B also survived the line's closure. It was purchased by CIE in 1958 and given the number 2509. The vehicle is shown here in this guise in CIE livery at Limerick Junction shed on 28th September 1974. Both *Lough Erne* and railcar B were subsequently preserved.** H C Casserley

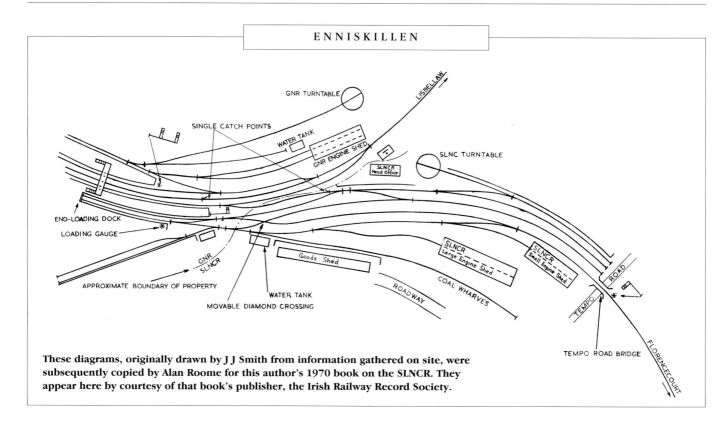

ENNISKILLEN

These diagrams, originally drawn by J J Smith from information gathered on site, were subsequently copied by Alan Roome for this author's 1970 book on the SLNCR. They appear here by courtesy of that book's publisher, the Irish Railway Record Society.

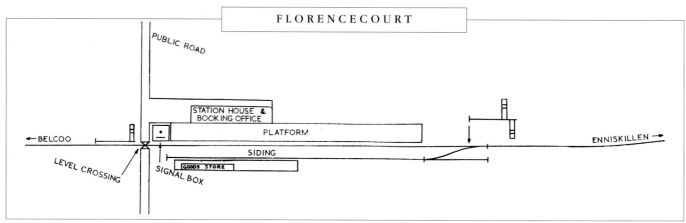

FLORENCECOURT

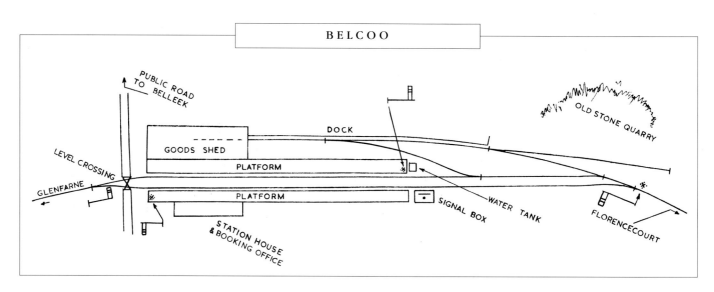

BELCOO

GLENFARNE

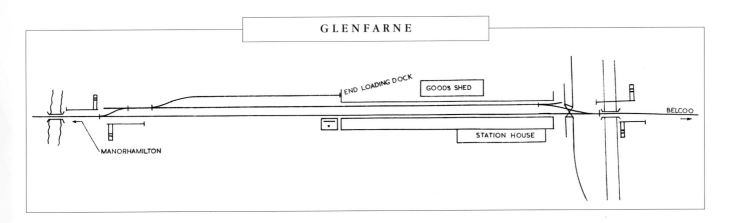

MANORHAMILTON

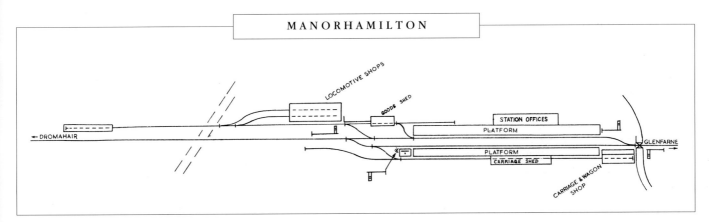

DROMAHAIR

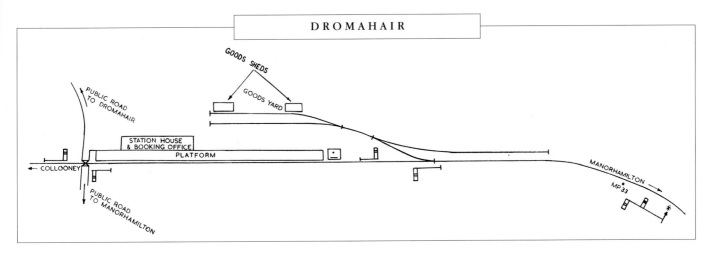

COLLOONEY

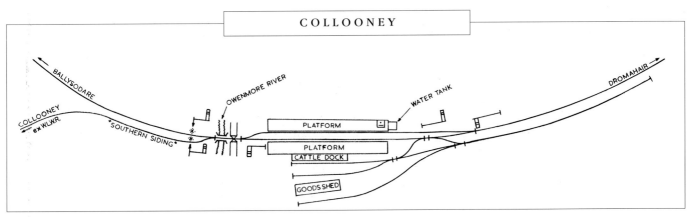

Top left: Two colour (black and red type) timetable poster for the Summer of 1938, the first based on two railbuses in operation. Connections throughout Ireland via Ballysodare and Enniskillen are highlighted as are tourist attractions in the areas served by the SLNCR. There is also an invitation to freight customers to consign all goods via Enniskillen, in both directions. All items in this section are from the author's collection, unless otherwise stated

Top right: **The 1951 Summer timetable illustrates the passenger service which operated for the rest of the company's existence.** The 6.20am ex-Sligo and the 2.00pm ex-Enniskillen (in later years 1.40, 1.45 or 1.50pm) were worked by a railbus and were followed, in both directions, by the main goods trains of the day, the 6.30am 'Livestock and Goods' from Sligo and the 2.30pm (or 2.15 or 2pm) from Enniskillen. The 6.20am ex-Enniskillen and the 4.00pm ex-Sligo were worked by railcar B which also operated the 9.30am Sligo to Enniskillen and the 12 noon return service which ran only during the summer. The 7.20pm Enniskillen to Sligo steam train was mixed, being the return working of the goods which left Sligo at 9.00am, later 9.45 or 11.15am. The passenger coach (usually No 9) for the 7.20pm was brought over empty on one of the two morning goods trains from Sligo. If there was insufficient traffic for the second goods train, it did not run and the 7.20pm from Enniskillen was operated by a railbus which usually worked empty from Sligo. In later years this occurred more frequently to the extent that the timings shown on this bill based on steam working, were amended to those for a railbus with an advertised arrival at Sligo of 9.35pm or thereabouts.

Left: **A poster for a typical Sunday excursion, in this case for football matches in Sligo on 13th May 1956.**

Sligo, Leitrim & Northern Counties Railway Company.

NOTICE

Of closing down of Rail and Road Services.

Consequent on the decision to close down the Great Northern Railway lines through Enniskillen as on and from 1st October, 1957, this Company will be unable to operate its services after 30th. September, 1957, and Notice is hereby given of the closing down of all Rail and Road services operated by this Company after that date.

No Passengers, Merchandise or Live Stock traffic will be accepted at any of the Company's Stations, including Sligo, Ballysodare and Enniskillen, which cannot reach its destination before midnight on Monday, 30th September.

All Merchandise on hands at Stations must be taken delivery of by consignees not later than Wednesday evening, 2nd October, 1957, and clearance of goods under Custom detention effected not later than same date.

By order of the Board,

Enniskillen,   E. W. MONAHAN,
20th. September, 1957.   Secretary & Gen. Manager.

Above: A poster announcing the closure of SLNCR rail and road services which was issued only on 20th September 1957, just ten days before the event occurred. As late as 18th September a meeting had taken place with the government of Northern Ireland concerning the line's future. This had proved fruitless and thus the fate of the SLNCR was sealed.

Right reading from top to bottom:
An enamel notice warning against trespass. R E Davis was SLNCR Secretary from 1877 to 1908. This notice was photographed at Belcoo on 18th April 1955. Richard Casserley

This, 'Look In Both Directions' enamel notice, recorded on 30th May 1954, was affixed to the fencing at the rear of the platform at Enniskillen which housed the SLNCR General and Traffic Managers' offices. This particular notice was aimed at SLNCR employees and perhaps visitors to the offices intending to cross the tracks to get to the GNR station.

These SLNCR notices dating from 1922 were still on display at Manorhamilton in September 1957, the month the line closed. The name of the current, since 1956, General Manager and Secretary, E W Monahan, has been superimposed over that of S C Little who had held the post from 1921. The notice on the left relates to the conditions of carriage of goods on rail, sea or canal transits. The one in the middle lists penalties for various misdemeanours. A £20 penalty awaited those who sent by rail, without notice to the company, aquafortis, oil of vitriol, gunpowder, lucifer matches or any other goods liable to combustion or of a dangerous nature. 'Wilfully setting fire to any station' was one of many acts which could lead to penal servitude for life or other severe punishments. The notice on the right was less threatening, dealing with the conditions and charges for the conveyance of parcels, goods and livestock traffic. Keith Walton

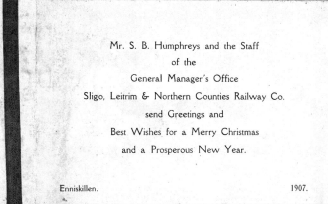

Mr. S. B. Humphreys and the Staff
of the
General Manager's Office
Sligo, Leitrim & Northern Counties Railway Co.
send Greetings and
Best Wishes for a Merry Christmas
and a Prosperous New Year.

Enniskillen.   1907.

Above: **A Christmas card dated 1907, produced for the SLNCR General Manager's office, with an illustration of the Weir's Bridge near Enniskillen on the front.** H Taylor collection

Sligo, Leitrim and Northern Counties Railway Company

No...............

FIRST CLASS FREE PASS

Issued to

Available
BETWEEN ALL STATIONS
DURING THE YEAR 1954
NOT TRANSFERABLE

This Free Pass is granted upon the understanding that the Company is not to be liable for any delay or injury to the person or property of the holder, and the use of the pass shall be deemed conclusive evidence of an agreement to that effect. The Holder is subject to the same Rules and Regulations as other Passengers.

Secretary and Gen. Manager.

SLIGO, LEITRIM, & NORTHERN
COUNTIES RAILWAY.

FREE PASS.
FIRST CLASS.

S. L. & N. C. Rly.

FIRST CLASS

LUGGAGE TICKET

Left and below: **A selection of leather passes including one for luggage and another for a commercial traveller's luggage and samples, in addition to the more usual travel passes.** H Taylor collection

---

Sligo, Leitrim & Northern Counties
Railway.

COMMERCIAL TRAVELLER'S LUGGAGE
AND SAMPLES TICKET.

NOT TRANSFERABLE.

No. 4

Available to 31st Dec. 1917

Mr. T. Cummins

Representing Zsad Buovik
Dublin

having signed the usual Risk Note is entitled to carry on this Company's Line **15 Cwt.** gross when travelling on a **First** Class Ticket

T. A. ARMSTRONG,
General Manager.

Sligo, Leitrim, & Northern Counties Railway.

No. **31**

FREE PASS. 1908. (FIRST CLASS.)

FRANK ROGERS, Esq.,
Belfast Steamship Company.
Between any Station and any Station.
NOT TRANSFERABLE.

This Free Pass is granted upon the understanding that the Company is not to be liable for any delay or injury to the person or property of the holder, and the use of the Pass shall be deemed conclusive evidence of an agreement to that effect. The Holder is subject to the same Rules and Regulations as other Passengers.

General Manager.

SLIGO, LEITRIM, AND
NORTHERN COUNTIES RAILWAY.

Free Pass.

FIRST CLASS.

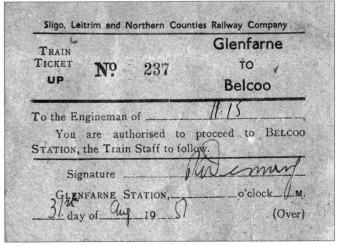

Above: **The cover of the 32 page timetable booklet issued for the final phase of services, the Summer of 1957. For many years the SLNCR had issued only timetable posters and this booklet seems to have been produced as a final fling. In addition to SLNCR train times and those of the principal bus services run by the company, the booklet showed connections with the GNR and CIE and numerous through connections by sea to and from Britain via Glasgow, Heysham, Holyhead, Liverpool and Stranraer. There were also numerous advertisements for local businesses. The photographs on the two colour (black and green) front cover, show railcar B entering Belcoo and *Lough Erne* leaving Florencecourt, and were taken by the present author.** Peter Hay collection

Top right: **A selection of SLNCR tickets. In the early years the basic colours for single tickets were white for First class, blue Second class and straw Third class. Full rate returns were yellow, pink and green, respectively. In the first two decades of the twentieth century two-colour returns were issued. Later the company reverted to single-colour tickets, yellow for First class, pink for Second class and a very pale buff for Third class.** John Langford collection

Centre: **A selection of SLNCR luggage labels for destinations both on and off their system.** Les Dench and John Langford collections

Lower right: **A ticket authorising the driver of the 11.15am Sligo to Enniskillen goods on 31st August 1957, to proceed from Glenfarne to Belcoo. The driver would have been shown the train staff which would follow in the possession of the driver of the 4.00pm Sligo to Enniskillen railcar.** John Langford collection

SLNCR BUS SERVICES

The SLNCR commenced operation of bus services on 2nd April 1945. This timetable bill from November 1949 shows the company's services at their fullest extent. The network of bus routes, as illustrated on the map below, remained unchanged until services ceased simultaneously with the end of railway operations on 30th September 1957.

The first SLNCR bus route, that from Blacklion to Sligo via Manorhamilton and Glencar, was purchased in 1945 from the previous operator, Appleby. The Blacklion to Sligo, via Dowra, Drumkeeran and Dromahair service, together with the school term diversion from Dowra to Ballinaglera, commenced on 12th February 1946. October of that year saw the start of a connecting service from Manorhamilton to Dromahair via Cloonaquin and Bohy. The final addition to the network was the service from Shanvas Cross to Sligo and back which operated from 13th May 1949.

These regular timetabled services were supplemented from time to time by excursions, and trips for special events. These included half day Summer Sunday runs from Blacklion to Bundoran.

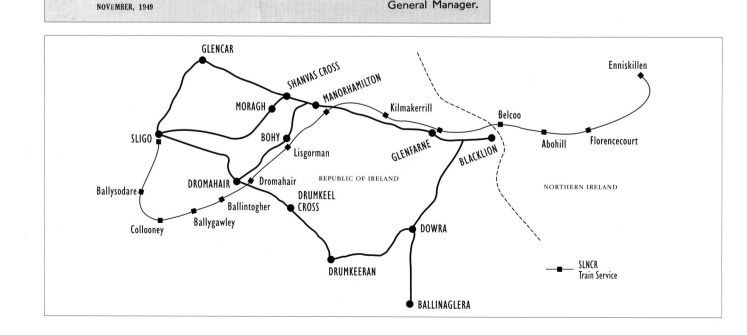